ZERO-BASE BUDGETING IN STATE AND LOCAL GOVERNMENT

ZERO-BASE BUDGETING IN STATE AND LOCAL GOVERNMENT

Current Experiences and Cases

edited by
John A. Worthley
William G. Ludwin

PRAEGER PUBLISHERS
Praeger Special Studies

New York • London • Sydney • Toronto

Library of Congress Cataloging in Publication Data
Main entry under title:

Zero-base budgeting in State and local government.

Includes bibliographical references.
1. Zero-base budgeting--United States--States--
Addresses, essays, lectures. 2. Local budgets--United
States--Addresses, essays, lectures. I. Worthley,
John A. II. Ludwin, William G.
HJ2052.Z47   352'.12'0973   79-10162
ISBN 0-03-049121-5

PRAEGER PUBLISHERS,
PRAEGER SPECIAL STUDIES
383 Madison Avenue, New York, N.Y. 10017, U.S.A.

Published in the United States of America in 1979
by Praeger Publishers,
A Division of Holt, Rinehart and Winston, CBS, Inc.

9   038   987654321

Printed in the United States of America

PREFACE

During the past few years, zero-base budgeting (ZBB) has attracted the attention of many state and local governments. Numerous jurisdictions have adopted it in their budgetary processes; many others are considering the use of ZBB. Despite this interest, there has been little written on the actual experience of state and local governments with zero-base budgeting. This volume is an effort to help fill that void: it describes and analyzes the actual experience of several state and local governments with zero-base budgeting.

The volume is written for practitioners seeking insight on the problems, benefits, and implementation strategies of ZBB. It is also intended for students of budgeting and of governmental reform who are interested in empirical study of budgeting-improvement efforts.

Many of the studies included were originally presented as papers at the 1978 national conference of the American Society for Public Administration. We are grateful to the conference organizers, particularly Professor Alan Steiss of Virginia Polytechnic Institute. The clerical assistance of Ms. Dorothy Franc and Ms. Martha Perry of Long Island University enabled timely preparation of the manuscript.

The study of public budgeting has, historically, suffered from a paucity of empirical evidence. This volume reflects our conviction that budgeting-improvement efforts will advance only if actual experience is studied, understood, and shared. We hope the volume assists those efforts.

v

CONTENTS

Chapter		Page

LIST OF TABLES AND FIGURES

ZERO-BASE BUDGETING

IN STATE AND LOCAL GOVERNMENT

1

ZERO-BASE BUDGETING IN THEORY AND PRACTICE

John A. Worthley
William G. Ludwin

Since 1970, when Peter Phyrr published "Zero-base Budgeting" in Harvard Business Review, [1] advocates of budget reform, from Jimmy Carter to the New York Times to chairpersons of large corporations, have been urging the use of this new form of budgeting known in popular parlance as ZBB. President Carter has required the federal bureaucracy to use it. The Times ran a front-page story on it that was headlined, "Zero-base Budgeting: It Made a Difference. "[2] Phyrr wrote a book that has sold thousands of copies. [3] Peter Sarant wrote another ZBB book, directing it specifically at the public sector;[4] and it, too, has been widely read. Even the staid Wall Street Journal has touted it. [5] All of which has prompted one observer to remark: "Medicine shows are back. Modern-day drummers are promoting zero-base budgeting as the latest snake-oil cure for financial ills. "[6]

Two things about this "snake-oil cure" phenomenon strike us as being remarkable. First, as a matter of historical interest, the recent hoopla over ZBB incorrectly suggests that it is a new idea. In fact, as far back as 1952, in what is still one of the best discourses on the concept, Verne Lewis wrote about, and urged adoption of, a new budgeting perspective. [7] He did not label it ZBB, but his idea was the same. Secondly—and this is what prompts this volume—most of these "modern-day drummers" speak of ZBB as a technique and instruct us on mechanics, procedures, and standard forms for implementing a zero-base budgeting system. They provide little insight on actual experience, particularly in the public sector; and more lamentably, in stressing ZBB merely as a technique, they offer a meager perspective on ZBB as a concept and on how it actually works within, and can be adapted to, public organizational realities.

This volume, drawing from the actual experience of state and local governments with ZBB, provides a more sobered and, we hope, useful picture of what zero-base budgeting is like in the public sector. As of this writing, 13 state governments (Arkansas, California, Florida, Georgia, Idaho, Missouri, Illinois, Montana, New Mexico, New Jersey, Rhode Island, Texas, and Tennessee) and numerous local governments (including Milpitas, California; Garland, Texas; Genesee County, New York; Grange, Texas; Salt Lake City, Utah; the town of Colonie, New York; and Wilmington, Delaware) have experimented with ZBB. The experiences in nine representative cases are recounted in the chapters that follow. This chapter summarizes the zero-base budgeting concept and chronicles lessons learned from actual experience in governmental units.

THE ZBB CONCEPT

The idea of zero-base budgeting stems from the classic dilemma of budgeting described by Lewis: "The $64 question on the expenditure side of public budgeting is: On what basis shall it be decided to allocate X dollars to activity A instead of allocating them to activity B."[8]

Lewis's approach was to think in terms of "alternative budgeting," that is, to weigh the consequences of allocating funds for one project and not for another. Zero-base budgeting, in concept, attempts to systematize the weighing of budget alternatives by clarifying the substance of various options and explicitly determining the priority of possible allocations.

Explanations of what zero-base budgeting is and how it is supposed to work are numerous. In fact, most of the existing writings on the subject are descriptions of the theory and procedural content of ZBB. The most prolific writer in this vein is Phyrr, who has condensed his book into several articles, including "The Zero-base Approach to Government Budgeting," which succinctly presents the basis of ZBB. [9] Phyrr describes the concept as an operating, planning, and budgeting process that requires each manager to justify a budget request in detail, from scratch, and, in effect, shifts the burden of proof to each manager. Phyrr's approach requires that all activities be identified in "decision packages," which are to be systematically analyzed and ranked in order of importance.

One of the best overviews of the concept is Graeme Taylor's article, "Introduction to Zero-base Budgeting,"[10] which explains the concepts, process, and techniques involved. Articles by Donald Harder, [11] Walter Broadnax, [12] Michael Granof and Dale Kinzel, [13] and Charlie Tyer, [14] are similarly useful.

In essence, ZBB is a way of thinking about organizational goals, activities, and resources that focuses attention on priorities. The process normally entails several identifiable steps:

1. clarification of organizational goals and objectives;
2. examination of existing structure, functions, and activities;
3. identification of decision units;
4. development of decision packages;
5. review and ranking of decision packages;
6. preparation of a budget.

The decision package is a statement of objectives, current operations, alternatives, and possible levels of funding for each decision unit. A decision unit is a subdivision of the organization (such as a cost center, a bureau, a program) that has responsibility for implementing a particular allocation. The studies in this volume indicate how these concepts and terms can be applied to specific enterprises.

The ZBB concept has been both praised and criticized on its theoretical merits. In theory, ZBB results in wiser and more efficient spending of tax dollars. James McGinnis claims that beyond the immediate effects of identifying inefficient programs, the process of developing decision packages produces better information and, subsequently, better management. [15] Phyrr prophesies that low-priority programs can be reduced or eliminated and high-impact programs increased. In brief, proponents have predicted that either money can be saved or programs expanded, that funds will be allocated more rationally and efficiencies accrued.

Skeptics have forecast less promising results, including the successful resistance to ZBB by old-line bureaucrats, [16] the development of paperwork mills, [17] and the inability to define clear objectives. [18] Robert Anthony has labeled ZBB a "fraud." He maintains it will not "zero-out" programs. [19] Robert Hartman believes a full ZBB system would be too time consuming to work. [20] And Allen Schick cautions that "zero-based budgeting by itself cannot override the much stronger incentives to seek larger budgets and expanded functions."[21] But all these comments have stemmed from crystal-ball observations. What has actual experience been in state and local governments?

THE ZBB EXPERIENCE

Experience thus far, as illustrated in the cases presented in this book, reveals that ZBB is by no means a panacea, but that, carefully implemented, it can produce significant benefits. A synthesis of lessons learned from experience with ZBB in state and local governments provides the following significant observations about its development and effectiveness.

The Overselling of ZBB As a Budget-Cutting Tool

Allen Schick correctly notes, "The overselling of new ideas is a chronic problem in American public administration."[22] It should be stressed that ZBB has not generally resulted in major budget cuts; but it has promoted redeployment of resources toward more productive programs. In the Georgia and New Jersey cases, some significant budget cuts were realized, but in the process, participants report that the greatest practical benefit was an improved sense of managerial direction. In Michigan, ZBB served to expand the budget, but, nonetheless, has been viewed as a significant advance because it improved management control and analysis. In nearly every case, ZBB seems to have stimulated the redirection of resources from less productive to more productive activities.

Dissatisfaction with the Old Budget Process

The city of Milpitas, California, in reporting a successful experience with ZBB, has found that a key factor was the city council's discontent with the old budget format.[23] Policy-making officials there apparently perceived a clear need for a new system for making sound decisions. In Nassau County, New York, a similarly clear perception of need existed in the Department of Recreation and Parks. Managers there were acutely aware that, as a "nonessential service" (the parks program), their agency particularly needed information and analysis focused on results and on sound resource management. They viewed ZBB as a useful tool for meeting this need and successfully changed their budgeting process.[24] And in New Jersey it was a clear fiscal crisis that prompted a successful application of zero-base budgeting.

A Multiyear Effort

The history of nearly every positive experience with zero-base budgeting is marked by a multiyear program of training, testing, and tailoring. In no case has ZBB been developed and successfully implemented in a single year. Both the New Orleans and Michigan cases, described in this book, illustrate the problems inherent in a crash-program approach; the Garland and Wilmington experiences show the benefits of an evolutionary approach. Zero-base budgeting, it would appear, simply cannot be installed and operationalized overnight or even over a year. It requires a continual process of modification, adaptation, and refinement. Problems and payoffs need to be self-discovered. Skills need to be developed. Information must be gathered. Resistance needs to mellow. And these things take lots of time.

The Need for New Skills

Zero-base budgeting presumes the availability of skills—cost-accounting skills, performance-measurement skills, and, most fundamentally, skills in defining objectives. As Donald Coleman observes, "What really is difficult and important is to get managers . . . accustomed to stating objectives and to organizing, controlling, and monitoring their costs toward the accomplishment of these objectives."[25] George Gruendel's analysis of the Illinois case presented in this volume clearly illustrates the salience of this guideline. Recognizing it, many jurisdictions have employed a management-by-objectives process, prior to instituting ZBB, as a tool for developing the objective-statement skills essential to a working zero-base budgeting system.

The Adaptation of ZBB to Individual Settings

Taylor argues: "There are almost limitless ways to adapt the basic ZBB concepts to the varying decisional needs of different organizations; . . . [ZBB's] basic principles must be adapted to fit each organization's unique management structure and culture."[26] We agree. The most successful uses of ZBB have been those that consciously tailored the development and implementation of ZBB to a particular organization's structure and functions. Concern about jargon is important. Training and forms employed should utilize terms familiar to the particular organization. Even such basic ZBB jargon as "decision units" and "decision packages" can and should be avoided when they cloud, rather than clarify, the thinking process.

The Need for Data

Just as ZBB presumes the availability of skills, so, too, it presumes the existence and availability of data—cost data, program data, measurement data. Unfortunately, much of the necessary data cannot be produced instantly. Information systems for generating, gathering, and organizing needed data must first be developed. For example, in Nassau County, New York, the introduction of management-by-objectives, prior to ZBB, produced, over the years, an information system that made zero-base budgeting informationally possible in the Department of Recreation and Parks. In New Orleans, failure to first develop needed data impeded ZBB.

The Paperwork Problem

A frequently voiced complaint about both management-by-objectives and ZBB is that they create a problem of paperwork, and that this not only abets resistance, but also tends to substitute paper shuffling for thinking. As Henry Goldman points out in his incisive piece, "ZBB Without Paperwork,"[27] the real advantages to zero-base budgeting come, not from the filling out of forms, but from the thinking that is developed through the process. Most successful cases are characterized not only by a requirement for putting objectives and performance analysis in writing, but also by concern over the paperwork problem. The organizations in these cases generally monitor the functionality of forms continually, to periodically revise them, and deliberately strive to make them concise and minimal in number. The South Dakota case is a premier illustration in this regard.

The Integration of ZBB with the Total Management System

Perhaps the most significant characteristic of the Garland and South Dakota cases is their integration of ZBB with a systematic management framework. In those cases ZBB was not introduced in isolation. In fact, it was implemented as a natural extension of a total management system in which overall goals, objectives, performance, training, personnel appraisal, and budgeting are tied together. This integration is made possible by a strong commitment of top management, not merely to the zero-base concept, but also to a progressive total management system. We consider this kind of high-level support and integration essential in affecting employee attitudes and in providing the training needed to achieve success with zero-base budgeting.

The above general observations are elucidated and elaborated in the case histories presented in this volume.

James R. Cleaveland reviews some important issues raised by applications of zero-base budgeting to local government. Those searching for a recipe for initiating ZBB will find all the ingredients for success in Cleaveland's study. By distilling information from a number of local government cases, he provides a summary of ZBB experiences in a well-organized chapter that covers the subject from the terms and mechanics involved to the politics. After defining ZBB's key components, he discusses an important and often overlooked topic—whether to implement ZBB or not. For those considering ZBB, this section raises important considerations that might be lost in the turmoil generated by a proposal to adopt the latest in budgeting. In the section "Questions and Answers," Cleaveland summarizes frequently asked questions about ZBB and provides answers developed from the experiences of local governments. His study offers answers not only to the questions he poses, but to many others dealing with the rationale and process of a zero-base approach.

The case study of New Jersey's Department of Community Affairs, by Michael J. Scheiring and Richard M. Anderson, is a penetrating lesson on how to use zero-base budgeting. The authors describe how ZBB in New Jersey is used as a management tool for developing priorities and controlling the budget. In spite of an accelerating budget, New Jersey was able to achieve control of its budget by allocating resources according to priorities established within the executive branch. Instead of the across-the-board cut approach, New Jersey officials were able to cut selectively and use the budget as a tool for squeezing maximum output from a controlled budget. Scheiring and Anderson report that not only the executive branch, but also the legislature, used the ZBB budget submissions as the basic documentation for decision making. Historically, legislatures have resisted changes in budgeting, but in this case a significant change in legislative reaction occurred. This case study of a successful ZBB approach reveals the opportunities for improved management and budgeting inherent in ZBB. Other case studies in this volume highlight problems to be avoided; Scheiring and Anderson display the results of success.

In describing the experience of the Illinois Department of Corrections, which in 1979 launches its sixth year with zero-base budgeting, Gruendel presents a case study of one of the earliest uses of ZBB. In tracing the development of ZBB since the fall of 1973, he describes the pitfalls, problems, solutions, and lessons associated with implementing a new budgetary technique. Of particular interest are the changes in the agency's use of ZBB over several budget cycles. Gruendel points out, with appropriate detail, how ZBB was modified to adapt it to organizational realities. In doing so he stresses two points also noted in other case studies: instituting ZBB requires trained analysts, from the beginning to the implementation process; and, as with any techniques for allocating scarce resources, some criteria for judging merit must be established. Public programs are particularly susceptible to problems of measuring output or value.

ZBB, much like other budgetary techniques, does not directly address this problem.

The five-year history of ZBB in the Illinois Department of Corrections provides a useful experience in adopting and carrying out a ZBB approach to budgeting. Gruendel's discussion strikes us as a valuable aid to both students and practitioners of public budgeting.

Glen E. Hahn, of the Michigan Bureau of Social Services, and Jeffrey D. Straussman, of Michigan State University, have analyzed the evolution or "drift" of the Michigan Bureau of Social Services to zero-base budgeting. Their case study demonstrates that ZBB is not a standardized technique implemented to cut the budget. Rather, ZBB in Michigan's Bureau of Social Services was adopted to expand the budget and to strengthen management control. While this use of ZBB is not typical, the case indicates that ZBB does not preclude budgetary increases. Improved management is a more typical objective and outcome. This case study of an unconventional ZBB approach offers some valuable lessons and insights.

First, an evolutionary introduction of a reform such as ZBB is likely to be met with less resistance than the wholesale adoption of a new technique. The peculiar budgetary environment in this case, which included a target approach to budgeting, attenuated potential staff resistance.

In addition a large portion of the budget in this case was "uncontrollable." This restricted the application of ZBB and limited its potential for affecting resource allocation.

And third, ZBB can become merely a tool for justifying incremental budgeting. If behavior roles do not change and outcomes are similar to what might be expected from an incremental approach, is ZBB any different from traditional budgeting methods? Hahn and Straussman report that better analysis did result, but the fundamental reason for using ZBB was to increase the budget. While the authors recognize that their case study does not validate the claims made for ZBB, they nevertheless regard it as a positive step toward improving governmental budgeting in that it improved management control and analysis. ZBB can be regarded as a success if expectations are lowered—and this is an important realization.

The city of New Orleans adopted zero-base budgeting at the end of 1976 and began a pilot program in 1977. Four departments, Civil Service, Fire, Health, and Streets, were chosen to carry out the pilot project. Edward J. Clynch has used the New Orleans attempt at ZBB as an opportunity to study the perceptions and roles of those associated with the pilot program; in doing so, he hopes to increase understanding of the budgeting process. Better understanding of the dynamics of implementing what many see as budget reform can help minimize problems generated by a change in the budgeting process.

In analyzing perceptions, Clynch highlights several potential problems that can be solved easily. Inadequate planning was seen as a significant problem, which tainted the entire process. It resulted in poorly understood instructions on doing ZBB and inadequate information for developing a budget document in a ZBB format. The result, according to Clynch, appeared to be that "a noticeable number of participants believe neither they personally nor key actors understand ZBB procedures."

Clynch's case study of ZBB participants gives insights into the relationships among various actors as they carry out a ZBB approach to budgeting. These insights are particularly valuable to those attempting to initiate budget reform, whether through ZBB or another system.

When the Republicans won control of the House and Senate in South Dakota on a "cut big government" theme, the first bill introduced in the 1977 session mandated the introduction of zero-base budgeting as a pilot project. Donald C. Dahlin's study is a thorough discussion of the origin, operation, and conclusion of the pilot project in the state's Department of Public Safety. By discussing ZBB in South Dakota within a political context, Dahlin provides an inside view of the dynamics of budgeting and the role ZBB played. With the political environment as a backdrop, the description of the implementation process comes into sharp focus. While ZBB is a system for allocating resources in a more rational manner, and despite the South Dakota legislature's direct interest in ZBB, the outcome was not significantly more rational. It appears that the Appropriations Committee did not use the information developed through the ZBB process. The legislature did, however, adopt a bill to extend ZBB to other departments. These seemingly paradoxical results may be interpreted in various ways, but the outcome is extended use of ZBB in South Dakota. Dahlin concludes his discussion with a set of recommendations for potential ZBB users.

He urges users to keep ZBB simple and flexible, and recommends using the current accounting systems and forms as much as possible. Defining terms and establishing procedures should not be accomplished through law, but by administrative action. His conclusion therefore is that ZBB should not displace existing methods, but that it should be integrated into the decision-making process. Dahlin notes further that unrealistically low minimum-service levels generate morale problems among those workers who would be eliminated if the minimum were adopted. He suggests that ZBB be implemented gradually. Implementing ZBB in a few agencies at a time has several advantages: operational problems can be worked out; enough time is permitted for a creditable effort; and training needs can be satisfied.

For practitioners and academics alike, the story of ZBB in South Dakota's Department of Public Safety offers numerous practical guidelines.

Among the earliest users of zero-base budgeting at the municipal level were Garland, Texas, and Wilmington, Delaware. Douglas H. Wilton, who worked with both governments in their implementation of ZBB, and Lewis McLain and Bruce Smith contrast the approach and experience in these two cases. They note that though they had opposite objectives—Wilmington needed to reduce expenditures while Garland wanted an orderly expansion of the budget—they both applied ZBB similarly and both found the process useful. Wilton, McLain, and Smith trace adjustments in the ZBB process made by each municipality over the years, and conclude that, in these two cases, the role and effectiveness of both managers and legislators in the budgetary process were enhanced.

Finally, the two earliest experiences with zero-base budgeting at the state level are presented in this volume as reprints of earlier articles. John D. LaFaver describes the effort of the New Mexico state legislature to zero-base programs. He identifies 15 major lessons learned in the experience thus far and concludes that the results of ZBB were neither as great as anticipated nor as minimal as detractors claim. George S. Minmier and Roger H. Hermanson present details of Jimmy Carter's effort to apply ZBB in Georgia state government, an effort that he continued in Washington. They point out both pluses and minuses in the Georgia experience and opine that on balance, zero-base budgeting served the bests interests of the state.

SUMMARY

The cases presented in this volume, as well as our study of other similar efforts, indicate that zero-base budgeting can be a useful and workable budgeting system in state and local government. It can be useful not as a "snake-oil cure," but as an aid in redirecting increasingly scarce resources to the most needed and productive programs. It can be workable as an aid to decision making if it is patiently tuned to, and integrated with, the organizational and managerial environment of each particular agency. Experience thus far indicates that a zero-base budgeting approach to government is here to stay and that it can indeed significantly aid officials and managers facing the fiscal challenges of state and local government.

NOTES

1. Peter A. Phyrr, "Zero-base Budgeting," Harvard Business Review 48, no. 4 (November/December 1970): 111-21.
2. Edward Cowan, "Zero-base Budgeting: It Made a Difference," New York Times (January 22, 1978), sec. 3, p. 1.
3. Peter A. Phyrr, Zero-base Budgeting (New York: Wiley, 1973).
4. Peter Sarant, Zero-base Budgeting in the Public Sector (Reading, Mass.: Addison-Wesley, 1976).
5. Wall Street Journal (March 11, 1977), p. 1.
6. "Does Zero-base Budgeting Work?" Peet, Marwick and Mitchell Review (February 1978).
7. Verne B. Lewis, "Toward a Theory of Budgeting," Public Administration Review 12, no. 1 (Winter 1952): 42-54.
8. Ibid., p. 42.
9. Peter A. Phyrr, "The Zero-base Approach to Government Budgeting," Public Administration Review 37, no. 1 (January/February 1977): 1-8.
10. Graeme Taylor, "Introduction to Zero-base Budgeting," The Bureaucrat 6, no. 1 (Spring 1977): 33-55.
11. Donald F. Harder, "Zero-Base: Federal Style," Public Administration Review 37, no. 4 (July/August 1977): 400-7.
12. Walter D. Broadnax, "Zero-base Budgeting," The Bureaucrat, 6, no. 1 (Spring 1977): 56-66.
13. Michael H. Granof and Dale A. Kinzel, "Zero-based Budgeting: Modest Proposal for Reform," Federal Accountant (December 1974): pp. 50-56.
14. Charlie B. Tyer, "Zero-base Budgeting: A Critical Analysis," Southern Review of Public Administration (June 1977): 80-107.
15. James F. McGinnis, "Pluses and Minuses of Zero-Base Budgeting," Administrative Management 37 (September 1976): 22.
16. T. J. Murray, "The Tough Job of Zero Budgeting," Dun's Review 104 (October 1974): 70.
17. McGinnis, op. cit., p. 22.
18. Jourdan Houston, "Zero-base Budgeting: Is There a Fad in Your Future?" The New Englander (February 1978), p. 45.
19. Robert N. Anthony, "Zero-Base Budgeting Is a Fraud," Wall Street Journal (April 27, 1977), p. 22.
20. Robert W. Hartman, "Next Steps in Budget Reform," Policy Analysis (Summer 1977), p. 389.
21. Allen Schick, "Zero-base Budgeting and Sunset," The Bureaucrat 6, no. 1 (Spring 1977): 12.
22. Ibid., p. 19.

23. "Does Zero-base Budgeting Work?" op. cit.

24. John A. Worthley, Consultant report, 1978.

25. Ronald Coleman, quoted in Houston, op. cit., p. 45.

26. Taylor, op. cit.,

27. Henry H. Goldman, "ZBB Without Paperwork," Management Review (October 1977), p. 51.

2

ZERO-BASE BUDGETING
IN LOCAL GOVERNMENT

James R. Cleaveland

A significant addition to the field of municipal finance has emerged in the last few years. Although this addition, zero-base budgeting (ZBB), originated in the private sector, it is equally useful in the public sector.

As it has evolved in the private sector, ZBB is a mechanism for budgeting in overhead or departments such as marketing, finance, and personnel, which do not produce easily measurable products. Budgeting personnel and supplies when production standards exist is fairly simple. The standards indicate the number of persons and amount of supplies needed to make each unit of output. Once the desired amount of output is known, it is relatively easy to establish the budget. Such simple formulas cannot be used to budget overhead activities, however.

Most governmental activities are comparable to overhead departments in industry. Therefore, it was not long after its successful development at Texas Instruments that ZBB was applied to government. The state of Georgia was the first government to adopt ZBB after then-Governor Jimmy Carter read about the experience at Texas Instruments. ZBB was first applied to municipal finance in Garland, Texas, for the 1974-75 budget and has been used there in each succeeding year. Since then, it has been applied, in varying circum-

---

James R. Cleaveland is a vice president with the Management Analysis Center, Inc. , a consulting firm in planning and budgeting.

stances, in at least 25 other local jurisdictions. The entire federal government was mandated to use ZBB principles to prepare the fiscal-year 1979 budget.

While much of the attention paid to ZBB has focused on its use as a cost-cutting mechanism, experience at the local-government level indicates that its use extends far beyond this major objective. Indeed, the key reason local governments have adopted ZBB is the desire to improve one or more weaknesses in the existing budget process.

Other than this general desire to improve the budget process, no other common thread runs through the local jurisdictions that have adopted ZBB. Jurisdictions ranging in population from 11,000 to 7,000,000 have implemented it successfully. Strong mayoral, council-manager, and commission forms of government have adapted it to their budgets. Jurisdictions with line-item budgets and those with modified-program budgets have used ZBB successfully. It has been applied in jurisdictions with and without performance-monitoring and evaluation systems such as management-by-objectives (MBO).

This chapter reviews some of the key lessons learned from the local-government applications of ZBB. It is not a cookbook explaining how to implement ZBB, but it does discuss how to deal with some of the major problems of implementation. Its goal is more modest: to help the municipal-finance officer understand ZBB and to evaluate whether it can be successfully applied in his jurisdiction.

The chapter is organized into four major sections. The first briefly describes ZBB's essential elements. The second describes some of the chief considerations in evaluating whether to implement ZBB. The third discusses the mechanics of implementing ZBB. The fourth answers questions the budget officer frequently asks.

ESSENTIALS OF ZBB

Three essential elements distinguish the use of ZBB: identifying and analyzing budget units; defining and analyzing service increments; and ranking service increments.

Identifying and Analyzing Budget Units

Most budgets are prepared and submitted by government departments, or by some standardized units (divisions) of departments. These units comprise the budget structure. This type of budget structure frequently proves too aggregative for ZBB, because many key activities are subtotaled under one division and it is difficult to study each one closely. The first step in ZBB is to review the current budget structure and define budget units small enough to allow close (zero-base) examination. The difficult part of this review is to avoid budget units that are too small to be meaningful.

A budget unit that is too large is a police department that groups traffic control, preventive patrol, and school-crossing guards in one division. To ensure a zero-base study of the budget, the division is best separated into three budget units. In some cases, activities are too finely separated to be meaningful. An example is the Parks Department, where a separate budget is prepared for each park. Maintenance of all similar parks can usually be combined into one unit for budgeting purposes.

After the budget structure has been defined, the next step is to scrutinize each budget unit's operations. The examination is built around answers to two questions: What if the activity were not funded at all; and are there other ways to perform the activity and meet the unit's objectives? The answer to the first question should lead to development and clarification of the unit's objectives. After they are defined, managers responsible for the activity and for preparing its budget must analyze and justify any proposed alternatives.

Defining and Analyzing Service Increments

ZBB assumes that even if an activity needs to be funded, it can be funded at a lower-than-current level and that less-than-current service can be provided. Normally, several lower levels of service can be expected to exist, although the budget unit's objectives may not be achieved at each level as well as it is at present. Determining which levels are technically feasible, and what the impact of operating at each of them would be, is the core of ZBB's second essential element.

Defining and analyzing service increments begins with defining the lowest technically feasible level of operation—that level of service below which it is questionable whether any expenditure for the budget unit is worthwhile. This first, or survival, level of service will provide substantially less service, in terms of quantity and quality, than is currently provided. Only the most important work elements at the lowest technically possible level of operation should be included. (The importance of even these activities must be justified as part of the process.) Naturally, the cost of providing a reduced level of service will be commensurately less than current expenditure levels.

The second and subsequent levels of service describe and justify additions to the survival level. They are defined in terms of the additional amount or quality of service to be provided and the resources needed to deliver it. Each level is justified on the basis of the additional benefits the organization will receive from the improved service. Normally, two or three optional levels bridge the survival and current levels of service. Levels above current service may be defined; they must also be described and justified.

The resulting plan is thus a series of optional funding levels from the presumed base of zero to and beyond the current level of service. Each level should be described in terms of increments of service and cost. The first level is an increment above the base of zero. The second level is described as the added costs and services above survival, and so on. Upper levels of management then pick a level of service for each activity by deciding how many increments of service they want to select for each budget unit.

Ranking Service Increments

The selection of a level of service to be funded for each budget unit is accomplished by ranking service increments—that is, the process of arranging service increments for all budget units in order of importance to the organization.

The process begins when managers of budget units meet as a team with their superior (ranking) manager. They review and discuss the relative merits of each service increment. The ranking manager is responsible for establishing an order of priority for each service increment in the division. Highest-priority service increments are ranked at the top of the list. Lower-priority increments are ranked in succession until all service increments have been ranked. The ranking is then transmitted to the next higher level of management, where the process is repeated. If necessary, the process is repeated at successively higher levels until service increments for the entire organization or jurisdiction have been ranked.

Since more service increments will exist than there are funds available, the chief administrative officer (CAO) must use the final list to fund service increments in order of priority until anticipated revenues are exhausted. At that point, the CAO draws a funding cutoff line. Those service increments above the line are funded; those below it are not.

Tables 2.1-2.3 below show how the ranking process can be applied to the safety, labor-relations, and employee-benefits divisions of a large city's personnel department.

Table 2.1 shows the safety division's identification of four service increments. The first three comprise the current level of service—five persons whose annual salaries total $63,840. The first in-

TABLE 2.1

Safety–Division Identification of Four Service Increments

Service Increment	Personnel Added	Added Cost	Program Consequences (per year)	
			Item	Number
Maintenance of state-required records; brief investigation of all employee complaints; investigation of serious injuries only	Safety director, safety inspector, secretary	$35,600	Injuries recorded	1,500
			Employee complaints	780
			Hours per complaint	2
			Injuries investigated	70
Investigation of all injuries requiring medication or treatment in clinic; identification of most serious causes of accidents	Safety inspector	14,480	Injuries recorded	1,450*
			Employee complaints	780
			Hours per complaint	2
			Injuries investigated	250*
Current level of service: increased extent of inspection of employee complaints and improved analysis of causes of accidents	Safety inspector	13,760	Injuries recorded	1,300*
			Employee complaints	780
			Hours per complaint	3*
			Injuries investigated	250
Improved analysis of causes of accidents and added some capacity to follow up on recommended changes in hazardous operations	Safety prevention officer	15,200	Injuries recorded	1,200*
			Employee complaints	780
			Hours per complaint	3
			Injuries investigated	250

*Denotes changes resulting from adding this service.

Source: Compiled by the author.

17

crement for this division is three persons providing minimum service. The second increment adds $14,480 to the budget (for another safety inspector) and increases the number of injuries investigated from 70 to 250. As a result of this increase in investigations, the number of injuries per year can be expected to fall from 1,500 to 1,450 because greater attention to investigating injuries would result in reducing the number of hazardous conditions.

Tables 2.2 and 2.3 illustrate how service increments for the safety, labor-relations, and employee-benefits divisions might be ranked. As shown in Table 2.2, a number is assigned to each service increment. The division head also indicates the cost of providing each service increment and the current level of service.

The three division heads meet with the personnel-department manager to determine each increment's relative importance to the entire department. Table 2.3 shows how that ranking might appear. Note that without significant expansion in the budget for a particular service increment, the number-three increment of the safety division would be eliminated in favor of the third increment of the labor-relations division. Note also that priorities for the employee-benefits division have been switched around during the ranking process.

TABLE 2.2

Cost of Service Increments

Safety (S)		Labor Relations (LR)		Employee Benefits (EB)	
Service Increment	Cost	Service Increment	Cost	Service Increment	Cost
S-1	$35,600	LR-1	$28,110	EB-1	$23,540
S-2	14,480	LR-2	8,660*	EB-2	12,920
S-3	13,760*	LR-3	15,950	EB-3	8,670
S-4	15,200			EB-4	7,180*
				EB-5	12,130

*Current level.
Source: Compiled by the author.

TABLE 2. 3

Service-Increment Ranking Table

Rank	Service Increment	Cost Increment	Cumulative Cost
1	S-1	$35,600	$ 35,600
2	LR-1	28,110	63,710
3	LR-2	8,660	72,370
4	EB-1	23,540	95,910
5	S-2	14,480	110,390
6	EB-2	12,920	123,310
7	EB-4	7,180	130,490
8	EB-3	8,670	139,160
9	LR-3	15,950	155,920
Current level of service			
10	S-3	13,760	168,870
11	EB-5	12,130	181,000
12	S-4	15,200	196,200

Note: S indicates safety division; LR, labor-relations division; and EB, employee-relations division.

Source: Compiled by the author.

CONSIDERING IMPLEMENTATION OF ZBB

The decision to use ZBB should not be taken lightly. Not only does the process itself involve more work in the first year than most other forms of budgeting, but it will also expose the decisions of managers and policy makers to critical public review. The decision maker who ignores these factors is apt to meet a great deal of resistance to implementing ZBB. Therefore, the person should determine that the gains from ZBB are worth the effort.

Four factors deserve attention when considering whether to adopt ZBB: objectives for the budget process, analysis of current practices, management-planning capabilities, and the management-improvement strategy. Carefully considering these factors from the very beginning will enable the jurisdiction to use ZBB to improve financial and program management.

Objectives for the Budget Process

Determining objectives for the budget process provides criteria for evaluating whether ZBB should be implemented, as well as for influencing the design of the process ultimately installed. ZBB formats and procedures for cutting costs will be different from those for improving top management's understanding of program operations.

The CAO and the budget officer should start by examining possible objectives of, or expectations for, budget improvement; several possibilities exist.

Rational Reallocation of Resources. ZBB enables rational shifting of funds from one program to another on the basis of relative priorities. When existing service increments are ranked, some low-priority programs may be ranked behind some new high-priority increments from other programs. Unless revenues increase faster than the inflation rate, the lower-priority increment is likely to be cut and the higher-priority increment funded.

Involvement of Line Managers. Since most budgets involve accounting exercises, annual budget preparation tends to be delegated to administrative or clerical personnel. ZBB, on the other hand, involves those managers who are responsible for delivering services. Because line managers are involved, three or four times more people may take part in budgeting.

Improvement of Organizational Development. Involving all management levels in meaningful budget decisions can help strengthen the management team's communications, teamwork, and financial management.

Lower-level managers learn about specific policies and priorities from their superiors. If higher levels of management disagree with a budget-unit manager's recommendations, ZBB forces the difference of opinion into the open for resolution.

When lower-level managers work with their superiors to rank service increments, all involved feel as though they have participated in making decisions that affect them. They may not always agree, but they have had a chance to state their case and they understand the basis for reaching decisions.

Line managers who have been involved in planning and preparing their own budgets can be expected to take increased responsibility for controlling actual expenditures within budgeted amounts. Increased responsibility for lower-level managers means that centralized, restricted control of individual expenditures can be relaxed.

Analysis of Budget Options. The justification of each service increment in effect provides a cost/benefit analysis for each level of program service. This information allows higher-level decision makers
to see the link between the cost of a program and its consequences
more clearly.

Comparison of Actual to Expected Performance. Each service increment in effect defines a level of performance for the budget unit to
attain. Properly articulated, the definition includes measures of expected performance. On the basis of these measures, data on actual
experience can be compared against expected targets to evaluate performance.

Analysis of Current Practices

Before a jurisdiction significantly alters its budget process, the
strengths and weaknesses of current budget practices must be evaluated. Proposed changes should, of course, capitalize on strengths
and improve weaknesses. The following items should be considered:
the nature of legal mandates, the types of information presented, the
use of forms, and the use of the computer.

Nature of Legal Mandates. A first step is to outline differences between the fixed mandates of state law and the more easily changed
local statutes.
    Many state laws require a certain format and fixed timetable
for presenting budgets. However, these requirements usually do not
prohibit alternate approaches to resources planning. Local requirements can be changed within limits, especially if the local legislative
body has been made part of the budget-improvement process. In either
case, it is important to understand the constraints imposed on budget
making by law and what freedom exists to modify the process.

Types of Information Presented. Perhaps the most influential factor
affecting the nature of the budget process is the type of information
to be included in the budget. That information determines how decision makers approach budget review. A budget process that gives decision makers detailed information on each object of expenditure will
cause them to act like cost accountants focusing on detailed costs. If
the budget includes detailed line-item costs showing increases between fiscal years, decision makers will spend their limited time trying to understand the impact of inflation. Program budgeting focuses
attention on changes in the costs of program categories.

If decision makers are to be policy makers and set priorities, they need other types of information. They must have clearly articulated policy options.

Most budgets obscure program and policy tradeoffs behind clouds of numbers. The way through this fog is to zero-base information collected and presented in the budget. Virtually every type of information should be analyzed to determine whether it is germane to the types of decisions to be made at each level in the organization.

Some jurisdictions include every position, and its cost, in the budget. It is doubtful that this information is useful to top-level decision makers. Therefore, these data could easily be left out of the printed budget. They could be provided instead on supplementary worksheets.

Other jurisdictions include detailed lists of equipment and supplies in the budget. This type of detail may be important to the CAO and to various departments for internal control, but the value of printing such schedules for the legislative body's review is questionable. Again, informal worksheets may be adequate substitutes for a printed document.

Still other jurisdictions break down, in the budget, proposed spending by minor objects of expenditure. Detailed object-of-expenditure data are necessary as a basis for financial control, but such detail obscures more program and policy issues than it clarifies.

Many budgets also present brief program descriptions; definitions of objectives, by department or division; and lists of program measures. Again, if it is not useful to decision makers in understanding policy options, the information could be deleted.

Use of Forms. Government generally involves too much paperwork. Jurisdictions tend to use too many forms, which duplicate too much information. Forms tend to become an end in themselves, thereby stifling thought. Each form should be analyzed to determine its necessity. Perhaps some forms could be consolidated to avoid repetition; some information could be presented on an exceptions basis, or information could be obtained orally during hearings.

Use of the Computer. Computers are both friend and foe. They have removed a great deal of drudgery from budgeting, but, if misused, they can drown the process. How computers are currently used and how they could be used should be examined before any decisions to change the budgeting process are made. Computers can be used most effectively for routine clerical budgeting work—itemizing salaries for the coming year, for example—rather than in situations where manual operations would be more flexible.

Management-Planning Capabilities

Budget systems are frequently designed to be smoothly functioning accounting exercises, which exclude program managers by being submitted at the department or division level, so that there is no built-in role for lower-level line managers; by concentrating on accounting detail; and by ignoring the concerns of operating managers.

Many recent improvements in planning and budgeting (for example, MBO, ZBB, decentralized financial accountability) require the close involvement of operating managers. Considering a new budget process requires assessing managers' planning capabilities.

A top-to-bottom assessment of management's abilities to plan and budget should ask:

1. Who has been responsible for these tasks in the past?
2. If line managers have not been involved, why? Are they incapable? Has top management never permitted them to be involved? Have they never been trained for such involvement?
3. What barriers stand in the way of involving line managers in planning, budgeting, and taking responsibility for controlling expenditures?

If line managers are incapable of planning a budget and controlling the costs of their operations, ZBB should not be implemented. Experience has shown, however, that when given proper guidance and assistance, few willing line managers are incapable. If managers are able but untrained and inexperienced, the strategy for implementing ZBB should call for extensive training and provision of technical assistance throughout the process.

The Management-Improvement Strategy

A final consideration in deciding whether to implement ZBB is its potential place in a jurisdiction's overall strategy for improving management. Budget preparation is a key, but hardly the only, element of management. Improving resources management involves other elements, such as the basic accounting system (and computer support), use of financial reports to control spending, review of program performance (MBO), strategic or long-range planning, analysis of productivity improvement, training in management skills, etc.

These elements are not mutually exclusive. Each should play a part in an integrated approach to improving the management of resources. Strategic or long-range planning leads naturally to the an-

nual process of allocating resources (budgeting). Performance review
and improved financial control should be based upon performance and
financial plans developed during budget formulation.

Major improvements cannot be made in all areas at once, however. Selectivity is needed. Therefore, as part of the decision to implement ZBB, top management ought to develop a two-to-three-year
resources-management strategy.

MECHANICS OF IMPLEMENTATION

After the CAO has decided to implement ZBB, eight steps must
be followed for its successful implementation: gaining support of the
legislative body and department heads, designing the process, training line managers, using program measures, reviewing submissions,
ranking service increments, presenting the budget, and preparing for
legislative review.

Gaining Support

ZBB is an arduous and time-consuming process; it requires a
great deal of effort from all involved. Unless everyone is convinced
of its usefulness, it is likely that attempts will be made to circumvent
the process.

One of the CAO's key roles is to sell the process to both the
jurisdiction's legislative body and his department heads. Legislative
concurrence ensures citywide policy support for this major management effort. It may not be difficult. Legislative bodies have become
increasingly active participants in budgeting. As knowledge of ZBB
gains greater public understanding, legislatures are more likely to
take the lead in encouraging its use. Some legislative bodies have
actually pushed for implementation of ZBB by holding hearings on the
subject or bringing in experts to explain the process. Since ZBB is
primarily a management tool, however, councils or boards should
avoid intruding too much into administrative concerns. The legislative
body can cajole the administration and perhaps offer to fund implementation, but it cannot legislate that ZBB be implemented by an un-
willing administration and expect a useful outcome. The legislature
best serves the beginning of the process by encouraging investigation
and consideration of ZBB by the city administration.

If the council or board is not the original stimulus, it should at
least be involved in approving the decision to implement ZBB. This
approval may take the form of an affirmative vote to engage an outside expert. It may take the form of a resolution supporting the ad-

ministration's implementation of ZBB. Whatever mode is used, the legislative body should go on record in favor of ZBB to support the CAO in his efforts in implementation. Involving the council or board also removes department heads' ability to end-run the administration and thereby foil the process.

Two caveats are in order, however. One typical dream of a legislator is that ZBB will produce the same services at less cost. In some cases, although nearly the same services sometimes can be produced for less cost, it is not likely that all existing levels of service can be accommodated in a reduced budget.

Decisions to reduce costs by cutting low-priority services are still tough decisions—decisions which the legislative body cannot escape making in ZBB. These decisions may, in fact, be more difficult with ZBB because the consequences of reductions are defined and highlighted so that they are difficult to ignore.

Besides obtaining the concurrence of the legislative body, the CAO must enlist the support of department heads. He must indicate his firm intention to use ZBB to make decisions. If department heads perceive a lack of commitment at the top, they may try to circumvent the process.

The CAO should first meet with department heads to discuss ZBB concepts. This meeting establishes top-level support for the process and provides department heads with some working knowledge before implementation begins. At this juncture, the CAO would do well to explain how ZBB can help department heads gain more knowledge about their departments' operations and budgets. Normally, this meeting can also be used so that department heads can voice their ideas about the process design. Making department heads partners in the design is a way to secure their strong support for implementation. Finally, the CAO can convey to department heads key program priorities or emphases he wants reflected in their budgets.

Designing the Process

Because ZBB is little more than a set of concepts, there are few instances where forms and procedures from one jurisdiction can be successfully plugged into another. Each jurisdiction must therefore design its own process. The task of designing the ZBB process usually is assigned to the chief budgeting officer or to an assistant to the CAO. Working with the CAO and selected department personnel involved in the current process, the budget officer must develop an approach to implementation consistent with local needs. If a thorough study of ZBB, and the reasons for implementing it, has already been undertaken, the design can be rapidly tailored to the jurisdiction's needs.

The selected design should be thought through in detail and documented in a manual to ensure consistent application of the concepts. The manual should contain sections on ZBB concepts, general procedures for the jurisdiction, and forms to be used and how to complete them, as well as an example of how to fill in each form.

The ideal set of procedures, or budget manual, will allow maximum freedom to accommodate individual approaches to analysis and to adapt the concepts to the peculiarities of each program. This flexibility is enhanced if implementation is staged to encourage relatively unstructured creative thought early in the process and a step-by-step documentation and summary of budget requests later.

The process designer should remember that, in implementing ZBB, managers who have never been involved in planning are assuming a new responsibility. They are being asked to adopt a different way of thinking about their operations. Do not expect analysis to be completed easily on the first try. Allow for trial and error in the process by requesting interim submissions for review and providing intensive assistance to those who are having difficulty.

Training Line Managers

Implementing ZBB is, at best, a difficult process. It requires extensive training of, and technical assistance to, line managers for two reasons: it is a new type of process requiring analysis of the total budget rather than additions to the existing base; and it involves managers who may never have had previous budgeting experience.

A fairly extensive training program, involving both lectures and workshops, usually is needed to acquaint line managers with ZBB concepts. But training by itself is normally not enough to ensure a satisfactory level of analysis. Direct technical assistance should be provided to each manager. Most managers find it relatively easy to see how zero-base analysis applies to someone else's operation, but they usually have trouble applying it to their own operations. Personalized assistance by someone outside the agency is normally required. The budget staff may be able to help provide outside assistance by working closely with each manager as he undertakes his analysis. They can help clarify objectives, alternatives, service levels, and justifications. However, they should not dictate the precise form of analysis, acting instead to raise questions, be the devil's advocate, and interpret the instructions.

Using Program Measures

More than other budget systems, ZBB depends upon program measures to indicate the results of analysis. However, they have been debated widely in academic circles; unfortunately, in practice, the use of measures has tended to become an end in itself—something to toss into the budget because the latest budget fad seems to require them.

Program measures are an integral part of the ZBB process because they help characterize service increments. Traditional budget justifications are often couched in words such as "more," "better," "increased," or "reduced." Program measures make justifications more specific. They attempt to quantify what top management buys by funding each service increment.

A number of different types of measures might be used to characterize service increments:

1. The context in which an activity operates—e. g. , number of households where trash must be collected, number of youths potentially using recreation facilities.
2. The nature of work done—its quality (frequency of maintenance, response times, hours of opening, etc.); its quantity (numbers of persons treated/served, miles of streets repaired, etc.); its inputs (hours of coverage or availability of services, amount of time available per task, number of fire units available for response, etc.).
3. The performance—e. g. , number of collections missed, error rates.
4. The impact—e. g. , reduced incidence of tooth decay, increased earnings of trainees.

Each measure, except those that relate to program context, is susceptible to change as a budget unit adds service increments. By observing how program measures change with each logical increment of funding for a budget unit, top management is provided with a practical, if somewhat unsophisticated, cost/benefit analysis. While managers must often rely upon estimates of program measures, what they lack in academic elegance, they make up for in practical value. Managers begin to think specifically in terms of performance targets and the impact of their actions; even if measures are estimates, a reasonably accurate estimate is usually better than imprecise words normally used. The person making the estimate is normally the one responsible for the activity and, therefore, the one most familiar with it. Moreover, there are checks against wildly improbable estimates. Such checks include:

1. Consistency: Normally, we expect that as the amount of dollars spent on a program increases, the economic phenomenon of diminishing returns occurs. The line manager's estimates of performance would therefore be expected to display this same phenomenon.
2. Departmental scrutiny: The process can be structured so that a manager's peers can review the estimated measures during ranking of service increments. The department head should also review and question estimates as part of his preparation for ranking.
3. Performance accountability: If the manager making estimates is expected to compare his actual performance against planned performance, he will be extremely careful when he makes estimates. On the one hand, he wants to justify his budget, but on the other, he may have to live with his claims.

Reviewing Submissions

As in any budget process, budget staff should review submissions closely to ensure that accounting data are acceptable. The budget staff can also spot policy issues for the CAO's examination. The review process described here focuses on the CAO's needs, but the same principles apply to the department head's review of his subordinates' submissions. This review has two phases:

1. Audit of accounting and personnel data: This step traditionally consists of checking the accuracy of the arithmetic, reconciling data with current totals, and identifying apparent "padding" of detailed cost data.
2. Review of service increments and departmental rankings: Staff members sensitive to jurisdictional programs and policies should undertake this review. Their role is to review service increments and rankings and pose questions about their logic: Are first increments as small as they can possibly be? Are low-priority items included in high-priority increments? They should also question departmental priorities: Are low-priority increments ranked high in the hope that they will not be noticed and therefore be ensured of funding? If departmental priorities do not seem consistent with citywide priorities, they should be reordered.

Ranking Service Increments

In general, there are three steps to ranking. Although the steps outlined below focus on the CAO's ranking, they are also applicable to departmental rankings. The CAO reviews and becomes familiar with departmental submissions; discusses submissions with each department head, either during formal hearings with the department head, his staff, and the budget staff, or during private conversations; ranks service increments.

There are many unjustified fears concerning the actual process of ranking service increments from different budget units. Conceptually and mechanically, the process is easy; making decisions, however, is difficult. Is an additional fire unit more important than an additional police patrol unit? ZBB does not make this choice easier. What it does do is increase the number of viable options and, thus, decisions to be made.

The more critical question is how to manage decisions on so many options. If one simple principle is observed, the ranking process can become quite manageable: Concentrate on ranking service increments in the gray areas, those service increments that are neither the highest nor the lowest priority. The ranking process thus becomes a practical, straightforward mechanism. Several other mechanisms can help define decisions to be made more clearly:

1. Staff members or deputies may perform an initial ranking of very high and very low priority service increments, thus narrowing the band of service increments higher-level managers must consider. Staff may rank top-priority increments totaling 85 percent of available revenues. Top management need only review them and spend its efforts ranking the rest of the available increments. Those above 110 percent of available revenues probably need not be ranked.
2. Managers themselves can perform this initial ranking by segregating service increments in three to five priority categories of roughly equal size. They need not internally rank the first or last category. The middle categories are then much more manageable and can be internally ranked one at a time.
3. Some jurisdictions have used a panel of deputies, department heads, etc., to score each service increment. The average score each activity obtains determines its rank.
4. Budget and/or departmental staff can package service increments from all budget units within a department into "super-service increments" for that department. These super-service increments are then ranked against those of other departments. This mechanism is less desirable than others because much detail is lost, management has less flexibility in making minor shifts around the cutoff line, and establishing super-service increments is rather difficult.

Presenting the Budget

ZBB may, but need not, alter the form of the budget presented to policy makers and the public. If the current budget is a traditional line-item document, it can continue to be presented that way. ZBB requires that line-item cost detail be prepared for accounting purposes, and the information is thus available for the presentation of the budget. A budget based on programs can also be presented.

In most cases, however, the budget's format will be altered significantly after ZBB is introduced. The change usually has been the inclusion of expenditure options (service increments) and the program justifications for each. There are two general approaches to presenting a zero-base budget—by individual budget unit or by rank order of priority of all service increments.

The recommended form of presentation is to present the analysis of service increments by individual budget unit, cross-referenced to the ranking table. All service increments are displayed by budget unit, within each department. Service increments recommended for funding are noted. The chief advantage of this format is that it shows, in one place, the optional levels of funding for each budget unit as a whole, thus allowing close program review during council hearings.

The alternative is to show the analysis of each service increment in the order shown on the ranking table for the whole jurisdiction. This approach makes it more difficult to review each program as a complete budget unit.

However, some jurisdictions have used it to emphasize to legislators that, when they consider and vote on budgets, they must make decisions based on interdepartmental service priorities.

Once the general structure for presenting information to legislators is decided, the next step is to determine how much information needs to be included. The volume of information resulting from ZBB is too great to be entirely useful to elected policy makers.

Some cities have chosen to present raw analyses of each service increment, submitted by budget units. This approach is useful when central-budget-staff resources are limited because it requires little additional central-staff time. However, there are two disadvantages: inconsistent writing styles may cause confusion, and too much information is presented.

The preferred approach is to present merely a summary of the information each budget unit submits. A minimal summary would include current funding for each unit; the proposed cost and number, of personnel positions for general fund and other funds for each service increment, and the cumulative total for each; an indication of which increments are included in the recommended budget; the citywide rank number for each increment; a one- or two-sentence description of the services provided and the justification for each service increment.

A more detailed summary might include the priority rank number for each increment within a department; program measures that characterize each service increment in quantitative terms; a list of alternative methods of operation that were considered and, if they we were not adopted, a brief but specific statement explaining why.

Either level of detail carries with it the disadvantage that it requires significant central-staff time to prepare summaries. The advantage is a more consistent and briefer presentation.

Preparing for Legislative Review

Before the zero-base budget is presented to the legislative body, its members must be educated about terms, techniques, and procedures. This briefing can take place either when the budget is presented or on the first day of budget hearings. Suggested topics include a review of ZBB concepts, the mechanics of the process, an example of the forms completed by a small department, how the CAO managed the ranking process, and how to use the budget format.

Council members' attention may also be directed to other special concerns:

1. Productivity: Members may wish to request a report on alternative methods of operation considered during the ZBB process and why they were rejected.
2. Performance Evaluation: Members might request periodic reports on measures of performance that are identified in the ZBB justifications.
3. Cutbacks: Members may want to know how staff will be reduced. In some cases, personnel may be reassigned from one activity to another; in others, staff may be reduced by attrition.

Council members may wish to begin their consideration by setting objectives for the budget review. These include reducing expenditures by a certain amount, selecting areas where they would like to see cuts, or examining detailed areas of critical concern. If they do not choose to set program or policy objectives, the legislators should at least agree to key rules of procedure before they begin review. The three most important rules are:

1. Avoid changing the ranking until public hearings are completed. This protects legislators from being stampeded by a persuasive speaker or pressure group.

2. Avoid the temptation to begin traditional line-item examination of the budget, in the hope of cutting a few more dollars from some items. Doing so ignores overall policies and priorities.
3. Concentrate on those service increments that fall into a gray area— those most apt to be eliminated if revenues drop, and those most apt to be added if revenues increase. To focus on clearly high priority items consumes valuable time that could better be spent discussing items council members and city administrators disagree about.

QUESTIONS AND ANSWERS

This section answers four questions CAOs frequently ask:

1. Need ZBB be done every year?
2. How much paperwork does ZBB involve?
3. What is the role of politics in ZBB?
4. What will ZBB mean to the budget office?

Need ZBB Be Done Every Year?

It is still too early to state definitely whether ZBB should be repeated every year. The answer is probably, "yes, but with some modifications." Continuing to present the budget in a ZBB format can hardly be prevented if the governing body wants to continue to see its expenditure options. Most cities which currently have more than one year's experience with ZBB have chosen to continue its use, but each in a modified form.

One of these jurisdictions requires total reanalysis of a budget unit only if there is a recommended program increase that was not presented the year before. Otherwise, the second-year process merely updates costs. The other jurisdiction may choose to reanalyze budget units but to consolidate the first service increments. The objective is to show only two increments between zero and the current level rather than the norm of three or four shown. Different departments or functions—fringe benefits, space rental—can be zero-based in different years. Federal government experience suggests zero-base analysis of program categories that cut across budget units or departments. Local government application might include zero-base analysis of all city activities meant to enhance the physical appearance or safety of the jurisdiction.

How Much Paperwork Does ZBB Involve?

ZBB is frequently accused of creating a blizzard of paper. Indeed, if all the data generated by each budget unit are sent directly to the CAO, he will likely be snowed under. (Any change in budget format—not just ZBB—will result in increased paper.) The real issue is not the amount of paper produced but the amount that the CAO must review and digest.

There are three ways to reduce the amount of paper presented to top management:

1. Eliminate some of the existing forms or at least ensure that certain detailed items are not forwarded to the CAO. Good budget office analysis should help here.
2. Prepare executive summaries for the CAO's review. This is a major budget staff function anyway. The CAO can thus review the summary and select which areas he wants to investigate more thoroughly.
3. Structure the ranking process so that the CAO must consider only a few of the service increments. Subordinates can rank highest-priority items before the CAO is involved, and the CAO can then concentrate on the gray areas around the cut-off line.

What Is the Role of Politics in ZBB?

The budget is a political document. Any decision-making process that calls for the exercise of judgment (rather than mechanical decision making) is inherently political. ZBB does not change this fact, but it can make the political process more efficient.

ZBB improves the political process by providing more information on which to base judgments. Each decision maker has detailed justifications for each choice and a clear picture of the priorities department heads have assigned. The more information legislators have, the better able they are to make sound decisions. In addition, the ranking process makes it more difficult for the lone pressure group to railroad its program through without scrutiny. Tradeoffs between pressure groups are brought into the open.

What Will ZBB Mean to the Budget Office?

As ZBB changes the nature of the budget process, it will also change the way the budget office operates and the relationship between the budget office and other departments. This change may be a mixed blessing; it depends on the personality and style of the budget officer and his staff. Many elements of current operations remain the same: The budget staff is still the process's referee; numbers and estimates must still be audited and questioned; the CAO still needs independent analyses and recommendations.

Other elements of the budget office's relationship with other departments will change significantly. There are three major aspects of the change:

1. The budget office actively helps departments prepare their budgets, rather than waiting until they are submitted and then reviewing them as disinterested analysts.
2. The budget staff becomes more heavily involved in program analysis, leaving commensurately less time available for detailed line-item cost analysis.
3. The budget staff is no longer responsible for making program decisions, although it can still make independent analyses and recommendations. Basic decision making now becomes the responsibility of those who operate programs.

Some budget officers have strenuously resisted ZBB—perhaps because of these changes, and perhaps because ZBB is an implied criticism of their function. Some mistakenly feel they have operated what is essentially ZBB for years, without calling it that. Others merely react negatively to the perceived change or diminution of their role in the jurisdiction's management.

There are a number of reasons why the budget office and budget officer should implement ZBB:

1. Because the budget office is not now responsible for decisions, it need no longer be the institutional bad guy or professional naysayer.
2. Budget analysts will have to develop close working relationships with line managers. To do so, they will need to develop an attitude of helpfulness. Two benefits are derived: Analysts become familiar with program operations and issues; and they will be able to guide and shape, though not control, budgets from the beginning of the process, rather than waiting passively until the budget is submitted.
3. The apparent power to control expenditures by line-item accounts will be replaced by the more meaningful ability to analyze and make recommendations on larger program and policy issues as they affect spending.

CONCLUSION

It is still too early to fully assess the impact of ZBB on local government. That it has been judged successful in many individual cases is obvious. Leaders of jurisdictions that have used ZBB have praised it, although those who have done the work have cursed it.

In most cases, however, ZBB has not resulted in the dramatic budget reductions of which proponents dream. It has been criticized for the amount of time it requires and the amount of paper it generates. Some of its critics claim that the term "zero-base" is misleading.

In assessing ZBB, it is important to remember that the process has been adopted for many reasons—reducing budgets; reallocating programs; improving top management's understanding of programs, policies, and priorities; enhancing management capacity and team-work; and monitoring performance. Therefore, no one set of criteria can be used to evaluate it. A few jurisdictions have used ZBB to iden-tify rational budget cuts. Others have been content to use ZBB merely to prevent tax increases. Most jurisdictions have reallocated some funds from one activity to another. In every case, top management and department heads emerge from the process with a better under-standing of programs, policies, and priorities.

ZBB greatly expands the number of line managers involved in the planning and budgeting of their programs. In most cases where higher levels of management involve their subordinates in ranking, a stronger spirit of teamwork derives from the process.

In the end, deciding whether to implement ZBB is a subjective judgment. Experience shows what benefits can be derived. The ques-tion is whether they are worth the effort. Each jurisdiction will have to weigh the pros and cons for its particular situation and then make the decision.

3

NEW JERSEY'S ZERO-BASE BUDGETING SYSTEM: A CASE STUDY OF THE DEPARTMENT OF COMMUNITY AFFAIRS

Michael J. Scheiring
Richard M. Anderson

Zero-base budgeting was instituted in New Jersey in July of 1974. This study traces the experience of zero-base budgeting (ZBB) in one department of the state government, the Department of Community Affairs. First we describe the overall budgetary environment of the state and the general background of the ZBB effort. We then focus on the Community Affairs Department's experience and conclude with observations on the implementation of zero-base budgeting in state government.

THE BUDGETING ENVIRONMENT OF NEW JERSEY

New Jersey is on a July 1-to-June 30 fiscal year. The state has a strong executive budget, established under the New Jersey Constitution and by statute. The constitution requires the budget to be balanced and permits the governor to line-item veto the Appropriations Act, as passed by the legislature. Item vetoes can be overturned by a two-thirds vote of the legislature. This gives New Jersey one of the strongest state executive budgeting systems in the nation.

In addition to the constitutional and statutory provisions concerning budget making, the New Jersey budget process during the

Michael J. Scheiring supervises the Community and Personal Economic Development Section of New Jersey's Bureau of the Budget. Richard M. Anderson is the fiscal and management services officer for the New Jersey Department of Community Affairs.

past decade has evolved from line-item budgeting to program budgeting to zero-base budgeting and contains elements of each of these processes, forming a hybrid suited to our political and historical environment.

New Jersey in recent times has been faced with a high unemployment rate, a stable economy, and an inelastic revenue base, yet it is still faced with high demands for services, particularly in such areas as education, Medicaid, welfare, and mass transportation.

A few statistics serve to illustrate this demand for services and increased state expenditures. In 1963, the state's expenditures were $500 million, and by 1969 they had grown to $1 billion. By 1973, expenditures doubled again and New Jersey had its first budget exceeding $2 billion. The budget for fiscal year 1978 was $4 billion. Thus, in a 15-year period, New Jersey's State expenditures grew eightfold.

This served as a contributing factor in the creation of another important element of the New Jersey budgeting environment—the 1978 enactment of an Expenditure Limitation Law, more commonly known as the CAP.

The CAP law places a limitation on expenditure growth for both the state and the local governments in New Jersey. On the local level this growth is restricted to a flat 5 percent and affects virtually all components of county and local spending. The CAP, as it affects state government, provides for expenditure growth proportionate to the growth of the per capita personal income of New Jersey. This growth for the fiscal year 1978 budget was 9.5 percent. It is expected that future years' growth will probably average about 7.5 percent. The CAP applies to all general state operations and capital construction expenditures. It does not apply to unrestricted federal grants, debt expenses, or state aid expenditures.

These are some of the important elements of the New Jersey budgeting environment that act to condition both the milieu under which ZBB operates and the aims of ZBB in New Jersey.

THE ZBB BACKGROUND

New Jersey's zero-base budget system was primarily developed as a management tool for the internal use of the state's departments and agencies and for the state Bureau of the Budget's use in developing the governor's executive budget.

The aims of New Jersey's zero-base budget system are:

1. to force all participants to focus on the necessity for choice as the key aspect of budgeting;

2. to require decision makers to combine planning, budgeting, and operational decision making into a systematic management process;
3. to force managers to quantify anticipated costs and to provide performance indicators on the need, effectiveness, efficiency, and outputs of the program;
4. to require managers to indicate to the budget decision maker the changes that would occur in the quality and quantity of the program outputs if funds were to be increased or decreased;
5. to answer the questions: How would the money be spent? What performance results would be expected?;
6. to indicate whether the current funding level is still justified, or if a lower or higher funding level would provide greater overall program benefits;
7. to elicit an indication from departmental officials as to where they would make reductions if the executive budget recommendations were lowered by the legislature;
8. to provide decision makers with the ability to examine and review program objectives and programs that were based on statutes enacted to meet problems or needs that were priorities of days long past;
9. to provide a means for questioning all programs; for focusing them on need, benefits to be derived, and costs to be incurred; and for ranking them with other programs, both old and new;
10. to provide a more rational way to control and reduce budgets.

Clearly, the aims of New Jersey ZBB system are predicated on the realization, alluded to earlier, that New Jersey cannot continue to sustain the state's expenditure growth rate. The demands for services, though real, have to compete for the marginal increases in revenue available, and permitted under the CAP law, for expansion of existing and new programs.

The ZBB forms used by most state agencies in preparing their budget requests are the Zero-Base Budget Request-Priority Package Form, the Zero-Base Priority Ranking Form, the Agency Priority Spending Analysis Form, and the Performance Analysis Form. These forms serve as a decision package, which identifies and describes a program activity in such a manner that management can evaluate its benefits and rank it against other activities competing for limited resources, and then decide whether to fund it. The forms are designed to provide management with an indication of the objectives of the program; the activities through which the program objectives are to be achieved; the benefits expected from the program; the quantitative and qualitative effects of reducing, increasing, or not approving the program activity; the expenditures of funds and personnel the activity requires; and the effect on personnel, resources, and revenues if the allocation of funds is reduced, increased, or not allotted at all.

For example, the Zero-Base Budget Request-Priority Package Form asks an agency to—

1. state the objective of the program activity;
2. list the legislative statutes that would need to be repealed or amended at the various funding levels: 0 percent, 50 percent, 75 percent, 100 percent, 125 percent, above 125 percent funding of the current funding level;
3. describe the qualitative effects or impacts of funding the program activity at the different funding levels;
4. evaluate the quantitative effects of each funding level on the program activity;
5. estimate the effects of each funding level on budgeted and committed revenues; and
6. indicate the effects of the alternative funding levels on personnel.

The information derived from this form attempts to provide answers to the central question of whether the benefits to be lost where funds would be decreased outweigh the benefits to be gained where funds would be increased or maintained. The answer is conditioned in part on the effects on what outputs (services, productivity) and inputs (revenues, personnel) would be lost or gained, and on the decision maker's subjective judgment as to whether the outputs and inputs are valuable and desirable. The judgments are made by various officials in the management hierarchy.

The Zero-Base Budget Priority Ranking Sheet serves, through a priority ranking process, to rank the budget judgments of management decision makers. The form requires the agency to rank the program activities within a program subcategory in priority order, at the various funding levels.

Utilizing the ZBB Budget Request-Priority Package Forms, which have required agency managers to describe the effects of various funding levels on performing a program activity, the state decision maker is able to compare and rank the decision packages in a manner that will be consistent with the desired objectives and that will seek to optimize the program's success in achieving objectives and benefits. The agency budget decision makers are then able, utilizing the ZBB Priority Ranking Sheet, to accept or reject a discrete level of effort and to know the effects of their decision. In essence, ZBB furnishes the decision maker with the information necessary to make a determination as to whether funding at a current, increased, or a lower level is justified by the benefits to be realized or lost by a particular funding level. It serves to answer the questions: "How much should we spend?" and "Where should we spend it?" The ranking process provides management with a working tool to evaluate and allocate its resources in a more rational manner, and gives them the ability to realign program priorities.

The Performance Analysis Form in the decision package serves to provide additional performance data on the outputs and effects of various programs. It provides historic and current data, and projects the effects of alternative funding levels on future-performance data. It acts to supply more detailed information on the effects of management decisions. It helps to make a decision, which by its very nature must be subjective, at least more rational.

How these forms are prepared and utilized by officials of the New Jersey Department of Community Affairs, in preparing their budget request, will now be discussed.

ZERO-BASE BUDGETING IN THE DEPARTMENT OF COMMUNITY AFFAIRS

The Department of Community Affairs budget of approximately 67 million state dollars is broken down into three main program sub-categories with a total of seven program elements. The subcategories and elements are (1) community-development management, which includes housing-code enforcement, housing and urban renewal, local government services, and state and regional planning; (2) human-resource development, including programs for using human resources, and helping the aging; and (3) department management, with its program element. The department requests appropriation for the 37 program activities that are included in the seven elements. Each element has a director responsible for several program activities.

The first basic step in ZBB is to develop the general program-activity objectives. This process involves the program managers, division directors, assistant commissioners, and the commissioner. The commissioner and assistant commissioners, through cabinet meetings, review of pending legislature, input from community leaders, and information received from the program manager and division director, rank the program objectives in priority sequence. This process of ranking the program-activity objectives is in reality based on the judgment of top department officials, on how they see the general overall needs of the public. Once a preliminary ranking of objectives has been completed and reviewed by division directors, adjustments are made and a final priority ranking is distributed to program managers as well as the State Budget Office and the Governor's Office.

Although working from a departmentwide priority-activity listing, the program managers in the Department of Community Affairs
play a very significant role in affecting policy-making decisions
reached at higher levels. The substantive data supplied for each decision package at the program-activity level focuses in greater detail
on the actual program-activity operations, including:

1. the legislative statutes that would need to be repealed or amended
   at the various funding levels;
2. the qualitative effects of funding the program activity at the different funding levels;
3. the quantitative effects of each funding level upon the program
   activity.
4. the effects of each funding level on budgeted and dedicated revenues.
5. the effects of the alternative funding levels on personnel.

Since the program managers primarily implement policy decisions from a higher level, the information supplied tells the policy
makers whether the overall objectives of the program activity were
satisfied as anticipated. This technical data must be accurate and reliable so the true results can be determined. The program managers'
decision packages, the division directors' recommendations, and the
department priority ranking serve to provide top management with the
basic information for determining funding-priority increments on a
departmentwide basis. Although judgment cannot be eliminated entirely in the agency priority-spending analysis, one can see that ZBB
has provided a degree of accountability not previously required in
justifying budget requests.

An example of the use of ZBB in New Jersey for the department's Housing Code Enforcement element is as follows. The program-activity objective statements cover the State Uniform Construction Code enforcement activities, designed to protect the public safety
by ensuring that all buildings constructed in New Jersey meet required
uniform construction standards as provided for by the State Construction Code, while benefiting the consumer through lower construction
costs; and housing-inspection activities, designed to preserve the
existing multifamily housing stock in the state and protect the health
and safety of the occupants of that housing through the code-enforce-
ment process established by the Hotel and Multiple Dwelling Law of
1967. Department management has ranked the Uniform Construction
Code enforcement activities objective number two, and the housing-
inspection activities objective number five in the department's priority-
objective listing. The program managers for the Uniform Construction

Code and housing-inspection activities prepare detailed decision packages. These, along with other, non-zero-base budget forms, are reviewed and approved by the director of the Division of Housing prior to being forwarded to the department's budget officer.

It is the responsibility of department management (the budget officer) to prepare the Agency Priority Spending Analysis Form, utilizing the information presented in the decision packages. The effects of different funding levels on the two activities are illustrated in Table 3.1 as they relate to the total department budget request, as projected on the Spending Analysis Form.

The Agency Priority Spending Analysis Form is the management tool for informing program managers as to various funding levels requested, and is their guide for determining the performance-analysis information. Performance-analysis information is projected in Table 3.2 for the housing-inspection activity.

Through an analysis of the performance-analysis information, it becomes clear what effect the policy decision noted on the Agency Priority Spending Analysis Form has on the operation of the housing-inspection activity. At a 75 percent level of funding for the department, management's decision is to reduce the number of units inspected. The qualitative effects, the statutes affected, and the number of personnel needed can be determined by reviewing the decision packages. Thus New Jersey's ZBB is designed to provide management and higher-level budget officials with the information needed to make budgetary decisions.

However, to determine if these budgetary decisions are based on accurate evaluation and cost data, we must examine the data collection and reporting system used in cost accounting and performance evaluation by the department as well as the state of New Jersey.

DEVELOPMENT OF COST DATA IN NEW JERSEY'S ZBB SYSTEM

When New Jersey established program budgeting in 1972, the state appropriation-accounting structure was revised to reflect this concept as well as maintain line-item detail. The state's centralized accounting system serves both as an expenditure-control mechanism and as a mechanism for cost identification by program element. The activity level is not controlled or costed out via the centralized system, and it is each department's responsibility to develop these costs in the best manner possible.

Being relatively small in size and computer resources, the Community Affairs Department has been forced to develop program-activity costs on an estimated basis, for use in developing its ZBB Priority

TABLE 3.1

Agency Priority Spending Analysis
(thousand dollars)

Program Activity	Fiscal Year 1976, Expended	Fiscal Year 1977, Appropriated	Incremental Funding Levels				Cumulative
			75 Percent	+25 Percent	+25 Percent	+ over	
Neighborhood Preservation	0	0	N/A	N/A	N/A	1,000	1,000
CC Enforcement	500	540	405	N/A	N/A	N/A	1,405
Housing Inspection	1,800	1,900	1,425	N/A	N/A	N/A	2,600
UCC Enforcement	N/A	N/A	N/A	95	N/A	N/A	6,095
UCC Enforcement	N/A	N/A	N/A	N/A	50	N/A	6,145
Housing Inspection	N/A	N/A	N/A	475	N/A	N/A	41,000
Housing Inspection	N/A	N/A	N/A	N/A	100	N/A	45,000
Department total	65,000	67,000	50,250	16,675	10,000	1,000	78,000

UCC indicates Uniform Construction Code; N/A, data not applicable.

Source: Departmental data.

TABLE 3.2

Performance Analysis

Housing Data	1976, Actual	1977, Actual	1977, Budgeted	Incremental Funding Levels for Fiscal Year 1978				Department Request
				75 Percent	+25 Percent	+25 Percent	+ over	
Units subject to inspection	165,000	167,000	170,000	170,000	170,000	170,000	170,000	170,000
Percent inspected	60	58	53	39	14	N/A	6	60
Cost per inspection	$12	$12	$12	$12	$12	$12	$12	$12
Units inspected	100,000	97,000	90,000	67,000	90,000		10,000	100,000

Source: Departmental data.

Package Forms as well as the Agency Priority Ranking Form. With personnel costs being a major factor in any activity, the department must manually distribute these costs based on assigned position titles and input from program managers. Personnel costs are not maintained below the program-element level and are among the most difficult to distribute fairly for purposes of ZBB. This time-consuming process results in delayed budget submissions as well as the possibility of understated or overstated budget requests that cannot be detected by higher budget officials because of insufficient centralized cost data.

A new appropriation-accounting system is now under consideration in New Jersey, with the aim of providing more detailed cost data. It is hoped that this system will provide reliable program-activity cost data for the annual ZBB as well as current cost data for monthly monitoring of funds appropriated from zero-based budgets. The delivery of this cost data by program activity, on a monthly basis, will allow program managers to determine the resource allocations that will best achieve the specified delivery-of-service targets. It will also provide division directors and higher department officials with the cost information needed to reallocate resources, as the need may arise, from one activity to another. This has not been the situation to date, except that the implementation of ZBB has demonstrated the need for better cost data that would enable program-activity objectives to be closely monitored to provide tighter managerial control over the delivery of services.

IDENTIFICATION OF PERFORMANCE-EVALUATION DATA IN NEW JERSEY'S ZBB SYSTEM

As indicated before, New Jersey embarked on program budgeting in 1972, and as part of this system, detailed instructions were developed outlining the steps to be taken in defining program-evaluation data. Department fiscal personnel and program managers were trained in identifying measures of need, effectiveness, efficiency, and output. The purpose was to provide detailed evaluation data in the annual departmental budget requests so that limited resources could be allocated to the most effective and efficient programs. Since zero-base budgeting had not yet been introduced, departments such as Community Affairs continued to present budget requests without detailed priority rankings; thus central budget officials were often called upon to determine the ranking of programs that ultimately affected the department's budget.

With the introduction of zero-base budgets, the state's Budget Office also introduced a program-objective progress-reporting sys-stem calling for a biannual progress report on selected program-activity objectives. The purpose of this report, and its timing, was to provide higher budget officials with detailed evaluation data concerning the current fiscal year. The due dates on the report are most critical since the first report provides data as of December 31, for the first six months of the fiscal year. With the annual budget message given by the governor during the first week in February, and the legislative budget hearings held during March and April, data included in this report can be very important for purposes of supporting the budget message as well as indicating changes from data reported early in the budget process. The importance of this system to ZBB is that the department is now operating with the data on programs outlined in the prior year's ZBB Performance Analysis Form and funded by the legislature.

In developing a program-objective reporting system along with, and based on, ZBB, the department has three main objectives: to aid in identifying and updating evaluation data that provide information on program-activity services; to act as an early warning signal for spotting developing problems, enabling program managers to make timely corrective judgments; and to provide a means of tracking actual performances and comparing them with planned or targeted performances. Activity-cost data at this point in time is not included in this reporting mechanism.

CONCLUSION

New Jersey's zero-base budget system is a workable management tool for decision making. The system provides the means for a department such as Community Affairs to identify expenditure options, document the consequences of these expenditure options, link the various levels of services with costs, and, most importantly, provide a means by which budget reductions can be made on the basis of priorities versus across-the-board cuts. To effectively use zero-base budgeting, department Management has had to make decisions and stand by these decisions during the budget process. The priority ranking of program activities that was submitted for the fiscal-year 1979 budget was reviewed by the state Budget Bureau and the Governor's Office, and basically funded in the same sequence indicated in the request. Out of $65 million worth of funded program activities noted in the governor's budget message, only $2 million in funding was different from the total requested by the department. The basic difference was the result of additional federal funding for another state department and the elimination of similar state funding for a program activity within Community Affairs.

For the first time since the department has been submitting zero-base budgets, the legislative Budget Office and the Joint Appropriations Committee used these budget submissions as a basis for questions concerning priorities and funding levels. This illustrates that with good documentation and devoted managers, zero-base budgeting can be used for decisions at all levels.

There are problems that still exist, however. The lack of detailed cost data, as outlined earlier, and the lack of attention to federal funds in the priority analysis are two major areas that must still be addressed.

Overall, the state's ZBB system has provided accountability for budget decisions and provided a more rational means of presenting total budget needs and resource requirements.

4

ZBB
IN THE ILLINOIS
DEPARTMENT OF CORRECTIONS

George F. Gruendel

The Illinois Department of Corrections adopted the zero-base budgeting (ZBB) concept as a program-budgeting technique and management tool in the fall of 1973. Following Texas Instruments and the state of Georgia, Illinois Corrections is, historically, the third most senior user of zero-base budgeting. The department has utilized this management tool in its endeavor to justify funding increases essential to providing a humane environment and program services for its spiraling residential population. This chapter describes and analyzes the department's experience to date.

OVERVIEW OF ILLINOIS CORRECTIONS

The Illinois Department of Corrections was created by an act of the 76th General Assembly and became operational on January 1, 1970. To serve adult offenders, the department now operates ten correctional institutions, which provide educational, vocational, medical, residential, and counseling services; and 18 small community correctional centers serving those nearing release; after-care supervision is provided for mandatory releasees and parolees. Institutional care is provided for juveniles at seven institutional facilities, while a continuum of community-oriented services, such as counseling, job replacement, medical service, and alternatives to traditional institu-

George F. Gruendel is manager of the Management Services Section of the Illinois Department of Corrections.

tional placement are offered in the department's four service regions by the Juvenile Field Services section.

The following statistics provide an overview of the department's resources and institutional population:

Resources (millions)	Fiscal Year (FY) 1973	FY/ 1974	FY/ 1975	FY/ 1976	FY/ 1977	FY/ 1978
Appropriation	$71.7	75.8	79.5	92.5	99.1	120.8

Average Daily Institutional Population	FY 1973/74	FY/1975	FY/1976	FY/1977
Juvenile	956	855	805	800
Adult	5,975	6,646	8,062	10,295
Total	6,931	7,501	8,867	11,095

The annual report issued by the Illinois Department of Corrections for 1973-74 acknowledged the department's adoption of ZBB as part of a corporate management model of operations. The report stated:

> Adult correctional institutions have historically been based on the medical management system, i.e., that which has developed in the Auburn (congregate) tradition and which focuses primarily on criminogenic (causative) client life factors, utilizing a prescriptive program delivery system. The four most basic operational impediments to the medical model are: 1) diagnosis has not been integrated with program decisions; 2) prescriptive programming by generic definition affords only minimal involvement by the client; 3) evaluation of prescriptive programming is virtually impossible from a management point of view because no standard is utilized by which individual programs are created; and 4) prescriptive programming tends to overemphasize the individual and his past life (causation), rather than his relation with his eventual reintegration in the free community.

> Because of these impediments, the Department of Corrections has chosen the corporate model design, since it utilizes a high incidence of private sector theory (organizational and functional management) in the development of the delivery system. It is believed that this is the first time that private sector management theory has been applied so extensively to corrections.

Another innovation is the introduction of the systems approach as a problem-solving technique.

The objectives of the Adult Institution Services Unit, which oversees the operation of the agency's nine correctional facilities for adults, are: 1) the refinement of the corporate model, establishing a standardized accountable system which can be evaluated by an objective systems-cost effective, cost benefit, research method; 2) development of the necessary specific resources to effect population stabilization in all facilities and reduction of the over-crowded conditions in the large, maximum-security institutions; 3) establishment of a rational basic program delivery system in each adult institution which can be cost accounted and integrated with the overall management function; and 4) introduction and application of various systems approaches into the management of the adult institutions.

Frequently, managers develop their plans and budgets by assuming the current level of operations and cost as an established base from which they identify only those desired increases from this base, thus looking at only a small fraction of the final budget dollars approved. This process does not require a detailed review of ongoing operations and expenditure levels and tends to be number oriented, rather than management oriented.

To improve the ability to manage effectively, the concept of Zero-Base Budgeting has been adopted by the Department. Zero-Base Budgeting is a general management tool that provides a systematic way of evaluating operations and programs, and which allows the potential to shift resources into what are considered to be the highest priority programs.

Zero-Base Budgeting offers numerous advantages to managers throughout the agency: 1) they have an opportunity to recommend how money should be spent; 2) they have an opportunity to evaluate their programs' effectiveness and to readily change their methods of operation to improve efficiency or effectiveness; 3) high-priority new programs can be funded by improving cost performance or by reducing or eliminating current programs with lower priorities; and 4) participation by managers throughout the agency will improve its management development, communications and discussions of key issues and problems. [1]

INTRODUCTION OF ZBB

The Corrections Department's first exposure to the ZBB process was in the spring of 1973, when the federal government began restricting reimbursement for services provided by various state agencies to those eligible under Title IV-A of the Social Security Act. As a result of this anticipated funding problem, Peter A. Phyrr was contracted to assist the Illinois Bureau of the Budget and the Department of Public Aid in applying ZBB to those programs which might be adversely affected by the new restrictions. At the time, Governor Dan Walker of Illinois stated:

> We've already begun exercises involving Zero-Base Budgeting. All agencies receiving Title 4A or Title 16 Funds under the Social Security Act face impending cuts for FY 1974 from the withdrawal of federal funding. I have asked them to systematically review and evaluate these programs and rank them. If programs are not funded, I want to make sure they are the ones which no longer meet the needs of people.

> This exercise will be extended to every agency and program and will be integrated with the other management reforms instituted by the departments. We have already completed the first stage of the implementation of MBO [management-by-objectives]. [2]

Staff Direction

Early in the development of the Title IV-A reimbursement program, the Department of Corrections created a Social Services Planning Unit, (SSPU) consisting of a director, two analyst/planners, an accountant, and a secretary. The unit's primary responsibility was to plan for and implement the provisions of the Social Security Act in order for the department to participate in the federal reimbursement program. When the governor, the Bureau of the Budget, and the Illinois Department of Public Aid decided to apply zero-base budgeting to eligible social services programs offered by the various agencies, this unit was given the ZBB assignment for Corrections. Thus, this one-time project became the agency's introduction to the concept.

The director of Corrections recognized the merits of ZBB and envisioned its application to the agency. The director decided to investigate the potential of the concept and the feasibility of introducing it to the entire Department of Corrections. The Social Services Planning Unit, because of the initial involvement with ZBB, and in face of the impending reduction in federal reimbursement, as an effort to justify and support its continuation, was assigned the role of conducting an in-depth analysis of the process and determining the relative merits of agencywide adoption.

The primary use of a planning- and program-oriented staff to direct the analysis, planning, implementation, and management of the zero-base budgeting process appears to be unique as compared to the use of fiscal staff in the private and public sector. The Budget and Fiscal Section of Corrections provided support, direction, technical assistance, and guidance in fiscal matters related to budget elements of the process. For example, they published instructions relative to the formula for calculating retirement and social security payments, and listed the items to be included in the major-object spending code— commodities, and so on.

In order for the agency to gain in-depth knowledge within a short period of time, a consultant was contracted by Corrections (as noted above) for a period of four months to experiment with the process, and, at the same time, provide training for the SSPU staff in ZBB techniques, in the event of a decision to totally implement the process throughout the department.

Pilot Project

The department decided to use the pilot-project approach. The objective of the pilot project was to identify and select a few key areas in which to implement the zero-base budgeting concept. This technique would also afford management the opportunity to identify and iron out problems prior to implementation throughout the department. The pilot-project method of introducing the concept would achieve the objective of expressing top management's commitment to zero-base budgeting, in addition to providing some staff with a first-hand knowledge of the process.

The department's approach was to experiment with the process at two facilities—a relatively small minimum-security juvenile institution and a large maximum-security adult institution.

The project was launched by scheduling a meeting with the juvenile institution's superintendent and the warden of the adult facility, and their top assistants, to discuss the overall project, define the purpose, determine the most feasible approach to employ, and develop a tentative timetable. Middle managers and decision-unit managers were introduced to ZBB through an on-site training program conducted by the consultants and the staff of the SSPU. Middle managers were trained in the techniques in order for them to be skilled in analyzing decision packages. Middle managers also demonstrated their support for the concept by showing a willingness to provide the time and resources to decision-unit managers for planning and budgeting. Decision-unit managers were considered the vital ingredient in a successful zero-base budgeting process and, therefore, received the highest level of training, support, and technical assistance possible.

The state of Georgia had a decision unit called Ambient Air, which was part of the Air Quality Control Laboratory. The decision was made to use this example in the Illinois Corrections Department for visuals and as a sample in the initial manual for unit managers. The consultant was quite familiar with the Georgia unit, the concepts of the process were well illustrated in the manual, and managers in the department could not copy the example for their specific unit. But the logic behind this was faulty. Many managers had not been exposed to state fiscal terminology; therefore, to introduce the language of ZBB through a totally foreign example was inappropriate. The department should have related the pilot project to the areas the staff were familiar with and built the concept around those areas.

During the experiment, a considerable amount of time was spent by the staff of the Social Services Planning Unit in providing on-site technical assistance to the unit managers to guide them through the process. This initial staff support also helped to reinforce the credibility of management's desire to adopt a viable management system through local participation.

The concept of utilizing the pilot-project approach in exploring the potential of implementing ZBB throughout the department proved to be extremely productive. Several vital facts were learned:

1. ZBB was compatible with, and complementary to, existing and planned systems.
2. The process would be an excellent device and a meaningful approach for the planning and budgeting efforts.
3. Middle managers and unit managers were enthusiastic about participating in the planning and budgeting.
4. Managers and administrators were quick to grasp the terminology and mechanics of the process.
5. On-site technical assistance would be essential in implementing the process.
6. The amount of data readily available to begin the process was limited, but adequate adjustments could be made initially without serious compromise.
7. Decision units are easily identifiable according to the existing organizational structure.
8. The previous and the current year's dollars can be identified by decision units with a reasonable degree of accuracy.

9. The forms were satisfactory, with only minor revisions needed prior to agencywide use.
10. The process reinforces good management principles and provides a means for developing managers.
11. To allow each decision-unit manager to identify the minimum level of effort for his unit, rather than establishing an acceptable minimum percent of the current year's allocation, initially would be a problem.
12. The resulting planning data and the level of fiscal-resource documentations would be more than adequate to satisfy the needs of the department, in addition to establishing a sound data bank.
13. Meaningful qualitative and quantitative measures will be difficult to identify, select, and define.

Policy Decision to Implement

Since the results of the pilot project proved to be extremely positive, the agency chose to totally implement the process in the fall of 1973. Specifically, the department selected the zero-base budgeting process because of the following reasons:

1. Zero-base budgeting establishes a common framework within which the organization's resources would be allocated rationally, provides a means for identifying and defining programs, and serves as a means for evaluating planned versus actual accomplishments.
2. Managers participate in identifying, planning, and budgeting, anticipated achievements for their area of responsibility.
3. Unrestricted competition for fiscal resources occurs well in advance of the date set to begin expending them—eight or nine months in advance.
4. Communications throughout the department are enhanced by the inherent need for managers to relate to their supervisor, colleagues, and subordinates.
5. The task of evaluation, initially, is delegated to the unit manager.
6. Management and staff development is a secondary benefit of the process.
7. Funding shifts are achieved rationally through the incremental ranking of decision packages.
8. Fiscal resources would be expended in a prudent manner according to a priority established through a logical plan.

ZERO-BASE BUDGETING FOR FISCAL YEAR 1975

Although the department decided to implement the process in toto for fiscal 1975, a few modifications were necessary in order to meet the time frames mandated by the Illinois Bureau of the Budget.

The decision to implement was made final in mid-to-late September, which, at best, afforded two weeks for the total plan of action to be developed, including the writing and publishing of instructions, printing of materials, and developing of training materials. This left about 25 days for decision-package preparation and priority ranking.

The Social Services Planning Unit was again assigned primary responsibility, but with this new assignment, came a new title as well—Management Services Unit (MSU). The staff complement remained the same, as did the relationship of the Budget and Fiscal Section to the process.

A major modification consisted of utilizing only six decision units for the institutions in lieu of the 14 that were used during the pilot project. This decision was made because fiscal information could be readily provided according to these units; the time required to identify the past year's expenditures and the current year's allocation according to the original 14 decision units was unavailable. An example of the modification of institutional units is as follows:

Modified Decision Units	Original Decision Units
Administration	Administration
Custodial	Business office
Medical and hospital	Clinic (counseling)
Education and vocational	Academic
Maintenance	Vocational
Counseling	Chaplaincy
	Medical/Psychiatric
	Recreation
	Security
	Dietary
	Maintenance
	Utilities
	Laundry
	Reception and classification

The use of six functions, or decision units, in some instances, forced two unit managers to plan and budget for a single decision unit. In many cases, the initial functional allocation of dollars was actually broken down further by the two managers to better serve their particular needs. As noted in one study of ZBB:

> The availability of data often constrains the choice of de-
> cision units. The organization's accounting system may
> not provide reliable cost data for the "ideal" decision unit
> structure. Compromises may have to be made, or the ac-
> counting system may be modified so that something ap-
> proaching the ideal structure may become feasible at a
> later time. [3]

It was learned, during the pilot project, that it took individual
technical assistance to question managers in order to talk them down
to a minimum level of effort that called for less than the current level
of funding. Lacking the luxury of time, the decision was made to force
the minimum level of effort to be at a "not to exceed percentage" of
current funding for package number one. The Department of Corrections's FY1975 General Budget Guidelines stated:

> Four program packages may be submitted for each func-
> tion:
> 1. Initial package totaling up to 80% of FY74 appropria-
>   tion;
> 2. Additional package bringing total up to 90% of FY74 ap-
>   propriation;
> 3. Additional package bringing total up to 100% of FY74
>   appropriation;
> 4. Additional packages bringing total up to over 100%
>   of FY74 appropriation. [4]

To some, this may seem to be an inappropriate approach, but
it does force managers to identify their priorities within the minimum
level of effort without having to spend a disproportionate amount of
time during the initial process.

A few appropriations should have been broken down into subap-
propriations, but time was not available for this. For example, three
youth camps were included in one appropriation. Each camp should
have its own appropriation, with at least four managers being included
within the appropriation.

Decision-unit managers were encouraged to develop quantitative
measures for their unit, but were also provided a list of the measures
from the pilot project.

Exploring and investigating alternative ways of performing the
same function was somewhat limited in the initial process because information was not readily available for decision-unit managers to estimate the cost and feasibility of recommending alternatives. In addition:

In the public and private sectors, the decisions to change often require additional study. For this reason, a great number of alternative ways may not be adopted the first time around. This comment is not designed to be negative, but one must realize this type of decision may affect a great number of people; and certain changes, unless done properly, and timely, could create an undesirable situation. [5]

Special guidelines, to help unit managers prepare data for the FY1975 budget, were published by the Corrections Department on October 4, 1973. The guidelines included: general information—approved functional units, funding levels (minimum 80 percent or less), salary guidelines, retirement and social security rates, and the date when the budget submission was due in Springfield; special instructions for budgeting for social services; and special forms and instructions for compiling budgetary information, including definitions of decision-unit terms, so that current fiscal resources could be allocated by unit.

As a preliminary step, the department felt it advantageous to have the managers compile certain information on a very simple form first, before tackling the decision-package forms. This would include information describing the purposes of programs and documenting what the manager would do at 80 percent funding—just the manager's first reaction.

Managers were also given the zero-base budgeting manual, which included an explanation of the purpose of ZBB, an overview of the process, definitions of terms, sample quantitative measures, and sample completed decision packages.

The instructions and training relative to priority ranking were purposely not introduced until the week before the budget submission was due in Springfield; the purpose, of course, was to minimize the amount of detail that had to be absorbed. Ranking can logically be separated from the preparation of decision packages.

The following represents the sequence of events that occurred during the original budget cycle for which ZBB was used:

1. Training was provided to administrators and business managers.
2. On-site training was provided to decision-unit managers.
3. On-site technical assistance was provided to administrators and managers; the director and two analyst/planners of the Management Services Unit provided extensive on-site training and technical assistance at the 27 appropriation sites scattered throughout the state of Illinois.

4. Special on-site training and technical assistance was provided in connection with ranking process.
5. Packages and ranking sheets were submitted to the General Office in Springfield.
6. Budget staff audited packages and ranking sheets for accuracy and mathematical correctness.
7. The Management Services Unit edited for completeness and to ensure the mechanics of the process had been followed.
8. Packages were returned for revision and correction, as needed.
9. Packages and ranking sheets were submitted to staff specialists in the General Office for their review and funding-level recommendations.
10. The department director conducted an in-depth review of the budget submission, which included his executive staff's presentation and recommendation of funding levels for those appropriations within his area of responsibility:

> The final decision level within Corrections is the Director's Review. The review involves the Director of Corrections and the executive for Program Services and Operations, fiscal staff, and the executive officer whose specific area of jurisdiction is being reviewed. Recommended funding levels, staff ratios, comparative costs, planned accomplishments, and so on, are discussed at considerable length, with the final result being a recommended funding level. [6]

11. The packages and ranking sheet were updated, as appropriate, according to funding.
12. The budget was submitted to the Illinois Bureau of the Budget for review and analysis.
13. The executive-branch funding level was determined by the governor and the Bureau of the Budget.
14. Packages were updated to reflect funding supported by the governor.
15. Budgets were submitted to the state legislature.
16. The legislature appropriated resources.
17. The governor signed the Appropriation Bill.
18. Appropriated resources were allocated to decision units.
19. Decision packages were updated to reflect funding.

LESSONS LEARNED

The FY1975 ZBB experience proved to be extremely beneficial, with the results exceeding original expectations. In order to set the stage for the approaching FY1976 planning and budgeting cycle, the director and the general services administrator decided to have the Management Services Unit plan and implement what was called FY1975, Phase 2. In early spring, when the appropriations seem relatively fixed, the MSU staff was to provide on-site technical assistance for the purpose of allocating the FY1975 resources according to the original 14 decision units. The final step required the unit manager to develop a decision package reflecting the allotted funding level. Thus, the plan was beginning to take shape for FY1976—the base (100 percent) had been identified for each decision unit.

As with any meaningful experience, many lessons were learned and, should the opportunity present itself again, certain approaches would be modified or changed completely.

The purpose of this section is to identify areas of concern or limitations experienced during the FY1975 cycle, recommend viable solutions or reasonable alternatives, and describe changes that have occurred in the department's system over the years.

The guidelines and instructions were adequate, but it would have been more advisable to develop a detailed manual for decision-unit managers. The department subsequently developed and published such a manual, which is updated annually. A manager's handbook should include:

1. General Overview—A general overview highlighting the concept of Zero-Base Budgeting may include such topics as the purpose for which Zero-Base Budgeting is being implemented; a restatement of commitment by top management; the goals of the organization; long range plans, and so forth.

2. Timetables—Timetables should specify milestones and target dates. The persons responsible for specific tasks should be identified.

3. Assumptions—In any planning process, a variety of assumptions must be addressed and communicated to those developing the plans. In budgeting, assumptions may include such things as inflationary costs; anticipated salary increases for employees; formula changes for social security and retirement system contribution; and other factors that are essential information for unit managers.

4. Definition of Terms—Defining terms provides managers with a consistent language and vocabulary. Definitions might clarify the kinds of items which may be purchased out of Commodities or Contractual Services. Terms

which are: <u>Minimum Level of Effort</u>, <u>Increments</u>, <u>Purpose</u>, <u>Consequences</u>, <u>Priority Ranking</u>, and so forth.

5. <u>Sequence of Events</u>—To provide guidance, particularly in the first year, a description of the various tasks the manager should follow in order to carry out the Zero-Base Budgeting process will prove to be invaluable.

6. <u>Sample Forms</u>—A section of the manual might be devoted to providing a complete set of blank forms, including decision packages and ranking sheets. Many managers may want to review the forms to become familiar with sections and experiment with them on their own.

7. <u>Sample Decision Packages</u>—A section of the manual should be devoted to presenting a series of completed decision packages that are relevant to the organization. The sample will serve as a reference for managers to ensure that information is inserted in the appropriate sections. It is desirable to provide at least two or three complete sample sets of decision packages representing different units. Each sample should include the minimum-level package and at least two incremental-level packages in order to demonstrate how the process should be carried out. Samples should also include the budget unit ranking, plus the master or integrated ranking of a number of decision units, as decided upon by the next level of management.

One pitfall that should be avoided is the attempt to use a completely unrelated budget unit as a sample. To use an example which is completely foreign to the unit managers may tend to develop an air of secrecy about the process which, in turn, presents an unnecessary obstacle to the implementation process.

8. <u>Miscellaneous Section</u>—A miscellaneous section is one that may be used for a variety of purposes, including such items as a list of names of persons to be contacted in the event that assistance is needed or a list of reading references for those who wish a more in-depth exposure to the concept of Zero-Base Budgeting. [7]

The three staff members of the Management Services Unit who provided on-site technical assistance were forced to deal with several managers to schedule visits, disseminate information and instructions, or answer questions. Subsequently, each institution, facility, and major unit has identified an on-site liaison person who serves as the local ZBB expert and contact person. The technical advisor's role has been described as follows:

> Properly trained technical advisors should be assigned responsibility for providing assistance to decision unit managers as they begin to implement the Zero-Base Budgeting process. In addition to providing on-site assistance and support, the technical advisor can serve as a communication link between the central office and an appropriate number of decision-unit managers. The technical advisor does not have the authority to bypass management. Assistance and support is the key to their role.
>
> In general, the persons selected to be technical advisors should be well-known, respected in the organization, have the ability to work with people, the willingness to accept a challenge, the capability to communicate openly with local management, and the desire to implement the Zero-Base Budgeting process as a viable management system. Insofar as professional training and experience are concerned, it is not necessary to select a professional accountant or planner. A person who is skilled in management techniques and possesses the aforementioned qualities should do quite well as a technical specialist. [8]

The identification and use of meaningful quantitative and qualitative measures has continued to be a major problem for the agency. It may be recalled that the approach employed during the initial phase of zero-base budgeting allowed each decision-unit manager to determine measures for his/her respective unit. A master list of measures, which had been identified by each decision-unit manager during the initial phase of zero-base budgeting, was compiled. The list consisted of approximately 300 different measures.

The next approach was to share the total list of measures with the wardens, administrators, and superintendents, and to request that they delete measures that are of limited or no value; add measures that are meaningful and appropriate.

The lists were returned and another master list compiled. Much to the surprise of the Springfield staff, few, if any, measures had been deleted, but at least 50 new measures had been added.

The next effort, which took place in 1976, consisted of scheduling a meeting of executive assistants to review existing measures and recommend revisions or changes deemed appropriate. Again, limited results were achieved.

In 1978 the department again resurrected the issue of meaningful measures—for the purpose of making another attempt at upgrading the quality of measures and more precisely define them in concrete terms. A reasonable alternative is to obtain outside consultant assistance—most management consulting firms employ specialists who are highly skilled in analysis techniques and developing performance measures. Additionally, outside development of performance measures assures objectivity and avoids the problems of in-house bias being built into the system. [9] The ZBB process also identified certain managers who were in need of management training: Unfortunately, some unit managers have not been afforded the opportunity, encouragement, or training to perform as managers. Therefore, ongoing training in management skills is often required to adequately equip "managers" with the skill to manage. [10]

The priority ranking of decision packages has created no significant problems for the agency. But one major tactical error almost occurred during the initial attempt at ranking the decision packages for all the adult institutions. The chief of Adult Institutional Services was asked to rank, according to order of importance, all packages, that is, one through, approximately, 675. Fortunately, the task was recognized as impossible before too much time and effort had been expended. More appropriately, he established a funding-support level for each institution after a thorough review and analysis of the packages, that is, support-funding packages 1 through 32, and packages 33 through 40, not supported for funding. As I have previously observed:

> As decision packages are processed up through the organization structure, it becomes less feasible to rerank packages. An executive who has management responsibility for a group of plants or institutions would be hard pressed to take a thousand decision packages and rank them 1 through 1,000. It would be a waste of time and effort to even attempt to do this.
>
> At this point, it is only feasible to review selected packages for funding and reranking decisions. [11]

A few years ago, the department planned to bring the management system to the level below the decision-unit manager—the employees. The method was to link the ZBB objectives and achievements to the employee performance-evaluation routine; the individual employee's performance objectives would be linked to the package measures, where feasible. Unfortunately, the plan was never implemented, but the concept has a great deal of merit:

The decision unit manager is responsible for the accomplishments specified at a given funding level. If the manager is to achieve these objectives, the employees must participate in the development and carrying out of accomplishments in order for the entire unit to be successful and achieve its objectives. This participation and involvement provides a golden opportunity for employees to identify the number of accomplishments they will be able to achieve as part of the total reflected by the decision package. These become the basis for an objective performance evaluation program for employees. Employees state they're able to accomplish "X" number of accomplishments during a given period of time and evaluation is based upon these stated objectives. [12]

The zero-base budgeting process has changed the management style of the department by involving decision-unit managers in the planning, budgeting, and accountability process.

In addition to being utilized for budget preparation and justification, the data from the decision packages provide pertinent data for the completion of the annual Illinois Human Services Plan, as mandated by the Illinois Welfare and Rehabilitation Services Act; form the data base for the agency's MBO program; and provide documentation for the governor's annual budget-accountability book.

In order to support the zero-base budgeting process, a few automated systems have been introduced. For example, a bimonthly payroll printout is generated, reflecting the current and cumulative expenditures for each employee, by decision unit. This report serves as a viable management tool for managers to track the personal-services status of his decision unit in comparison with plans and allotments. Expenditures in the other line items, such as contractual and commodity items, are maintained and provided by decision units through the use of automated accounting systems.

The Department of Corrections has just completed the fifth budget cycle using the concepts of zero-base budgeting, that is, for fiscal 1979. Like Texas Instruments, the state of Georgia, and others, the Illinois Corrections Department has revised and modified the process to meet organizational demands and changes. It now refers to the process as program budgeting; however, the elements of ZBB are retained. The same 14 institutional units used in the pilot program are now referred to as program units, and decision-unit managers as program managers.

Many corporations and agencies who use the ZBB concept have changed the title. Probably the most unique title is multiple-choice budgeting. Others include: resource identification; ZBB planning and budgeting; and resource planning and budgeting.

For FY1979, the decision package, or program budget request form, used by the Illinois Corrections Department was reduced from two pages to one page, with a few of the categories eliminated, such as "alternative ways of performing the same operation." Most other governmental and industrial users of ZBB have also eliminated the section after a few years; this has been explained elsewhere:

> Zero-Base Budgeting can and should be used on an annual basis. However, the task of identifying and investigating alternatives year after year may lose its value if no new alternatives become available. In this case, consideration should be given to eliminating this aspect of required decision package information. [13]

In the Illinois Corrections Department, the budget cycle for fiscal year 1979 was launched by the issuing of guidelines and instructions on September 14, 1977, along with a budget submission date of October 21, 1977.

In order to accommodate the changes in the 1979 process, the department prepared a revised handbook entitled Program Budget Request Handbook, which stated:

> The program budget submission serves several purposes:
> (1) It forms a basis for the review and evaluation of agency programs and supporting activities and their costs;
> (2) It links resources, priorities, and anticipated outcome of services;
> (3) It provides material for use in developing and justifying the Governor's budget.
> The major emphasis on the budget year (BY) requests of the Department of Corrections will be on programs and performance; therefore, units are to prepare and justify their annual budgets on the basis of programs and supporting activities. Data on anticipated accomplishments must be quantified and costs related to them in order to facilitate program and budget evaluation. The Director's emphasis on program accountability and evaluation necessitates the personal involvement of the program manager in the formulation of the program budget request.
>
> Meaningful quantitative measures should be used so that each function can be evaluated on the basis of anticipated

outcomes. So that all programs will be accountable to the
mission of the Department of Corrections, material from
"Description of Actions and Quantitative Measures" will
be used to formulate the agency's Management by Objectives plan.

The process for 1979 also set limits on the number of packages
that the managers could submit. Indeed, the FY1979 Program Budget
Request Handbook further stated: "Develop no more than six program
budget requests for each function, keeping the increments small (5%
or 6% of your total program budget requests)."

In the spring of 1978, the Department of Corrections, with the
aid of consultants, developed an automated system for tracking the
budget. The system tracks the request through the entire process—
from the decision-unit managers' preparation of the decision packages
to the signing of the final appropriation bill by the governor.

The budget-tracking system reduces the number of forms that
either the decision-unit managers and/or the institutions now prepare.
The computerized program automatically prints out such forms as the
decision-unit priority ranking; the master ranking (of institutions re-
ceiving appropriations); and cumulative forms (by package), giving
data on personnel, expenditures, and measures.

The decision-unit managers prepare a series of decision packages as usual. The warden, or the chief administrator of the institution's appropriation, ranks the packages according to priority and indicates the priority number on each respective decision package.

The decision packages are then forwarded to Springfield for
input into the computer. The computer subsequently prints out ranking
forms and other summaries, which include dollar figures and measures to be accomplished for each package.

The computer also prepares a number of supporting documents
essential to analysis, such as data on cumulative dollars, by object
of expenditure—personal services, commodities, contractual services—and by packages, as well as a variety of crosswalks to other
department budgets and personnel-related information.

The decision package continues to be the primary planning document and has also become the basic input document. Changes are
made by revising the packages and reprocessing them through the
computer, which in turn updates the ranking sheets, the supporting
documents, and other forms. The budget-tracking system should reduce a number of mathematical errors and save a considerable amount
of time in the field and in the General Office in Springfield. Plans are
currently being implemented to refine the functional-payroll system
and accounting system in order to provide timely and more detailed
information to all levels of management.

CONCLUSION

The Illinois Department of Corrections has launched its sixth planning and budgeting cycle according to the zero-base budgeting concept. Over the years, a number of changes, refinements, and automatic data-processing techniques have been developed to support the system and meet the changing needs of the agency.

The problem of identifying meaningful, measurable, definable, and controllable measures is again being addressed, which reflects positively on the interaction efforts within the agency to support the planning and accountability elements of the process. Indeed, the zero-base budgeting concept offers unlimited benefits when used as a meaningful management system that incorporates planning, budgeting, and accountability.

For the Illinois Department of Corrections, the benefits and advantages are apparent. This system, as with any management system, will continue to be successful only if those responsible for managing the system give it adequate time, attention, and resources. A management system does not fail unless management fails the system.

NOTES

1. Illinois Department of Corrections, 1973-1974 Annual Report (Springfield, 1975), pp. 16-17.

2. Quoted in Business and Commerce April, 1973.

3. Graeme M. Taylor, "Introduction to Zero-Base Budgeting," The Bureaucrat, March 1977.

4. Department of Corrections memo to wardens, superintendents, and division heads, October 4, 1973.

5. George F. Gruendel, "Managing Tax Dollars Through Zero-Base Budgeting," The Changing Face of State Finance (American Society for Public Administration, Central Illinois Chapter), April 1977, p. 36.

6. Ibid.

7. George F. Gruendel, Some Practical Answers to Common Questions About Zero-Base Budgeting (Springfield, Illinois: Dynamic Management Systems, 1977), pp. 64-67.

8. Ibid., p. 62.

9. Ibid., p. 27.

10. Ibid., p. 24.

11. Ibid., p. 49.

12. Ibid., p. 52.

13. Ibid., p. 33.

5

THE ADOPTION OF BUDGET REFORM: HOW ONE AGENCY DRIFTED TOWARD ZBB

Glen E. Hahn

Jeffrey D. Straussman

Critics of past efforts to rationalize the budget process have catalogued the various reasons why reformers fail. Allen Schick has provided us with perhaps the most complete list of failings through his autopsy of the federal government's experience with the planning-programming-budgeting (PPB) system of the mid-to-late 1960s. [1] Schick's list includes the following:

1. PPB did not become part of budget routines.
2. It was interpreted as a device designed by, and for, the Office of Management and Budget rather than for the departments.
3. It was unrealistically applied across the entire executive branch.
4. It is difficult to reconcile analysis, which produces conflict, with budgeting, which tries to suppress conflict.

The list could be extended. The few empirical studies of PPB, for example, showed that the success or lack of success of the reform effort greatly depended on top management. [2] Generally, PPB received, at best, a lukewarm reception from department heads. Finally, we could point to the obstacles to implementation when explaining why budget reforms fail. Here, the language of Aaron Wildavsky

---

Glen E. Hahn, formerly acting budget director in the Michigan Department of Social Services, is a doctoral fellow at Ohio State University. Jeffrey D. Straussman is assistant professor of political science at Michigan State University.

is most graphic: "The deeper change goes into the bowels of the organization, the more difficult it is to achieve."[3]

Such skepticism has, of course, not thwarted the efforts of a new wave of reformers, as evidenced by the current interest in zero-base budgeting (ZBB). ZBB zealots, for their part, have already been supplying the skeptics with ammunition. Robert N. Anthony, comptroller of the Department of Defense under Robert McNamara, has labeled zero-base budgeting a "fraud."[4] "Full zero-base budgeting would either waste the executive's time or be handed over to underlings and then be ignored," charges Robert W. Hartman of the Brookings Institution.[5] Recently, the National Journal asked budget officials in Washington about their reaction to the first year's experiment with ZBB in the Carter style. The Journal reports, "They were nearly unanimous in their views that the new system did not force them to dig deeply into their spending base."[6] Schick has even turned to poetry to sum up the most likely response that ZBB will receive. His last line of "Budget Gap" reads: So every generation's budget expectation ends up just another bureaucratic frustration.[7]

Undoubtedly, many of the attacks on past and current budget reforms are well aimed; nevertheless, it is difficult to separate the rather sweeping normative attacks from the much more limited empirical evidence that is available. The two have simply become hopelessly intertwined. In this study we make a modest attempt to do a bit of untangling. We take some of the broad criticisms that have been the stock-in-trade of the skeptics of budget reform mentioned above, modify the criticisms, and then implicitly examine the modifications with reference to a case study. Specifically, we suggest the following questions: What impact does the continued evolution of budgetary procedure have on the adoption of a particular budget reform? If the reform is adopted at a level below the department, will the prospects for success be improved? What effect does management support for a reform have on the implementation and impact of that reform? Contrary to Wildavsky's argument, is it possible to avoid, or at least minimize, resistance from program units within an organization when implementing a budget reform?

It is our belief that one useful way of approaching the subject of budget reforms is through a case study of a single agency. This type of micro analysis has not been sufficiently used in the study of budget reforms; yet it allows us to determine why a particular reform is adopted, how it is implemented, and what impact the reform may have had on budgeting within the organization. The case under consideration here concerns the adoption of a modified zero-base budgeting format in the Bureau of Social Services (BSS) of the Michigan Department of Social Services (hereafter referred to as the department) for fiscal year (FY) 1978-79. After describing the reasons for the adoption of zero-base budgeting in BSS, we then try to assess its impact. Finally, we conclude with some observations about the implications of the case study for an understanding of the potentials and limits of budget reforms.

THE DRIFT TOWARD ZERO-BASE
BUDGETING IN A SINGLE AGENCY

Critics of budget reforms like PPB or ZBB often juxtapose the reform procedures against an allegedly typical line-item, incremental budget process as a way of exposing the inherent weaknesses of the reform in question. Yet budget procedures evolve so that at any one point in time the process may actually be a hybrid—including ingredients of more than one reform. The pattern of change in budgetary procedures, nevertheless, makes the adoption of some reforms more likely than that of others. Our case study shows that the evolution of budgetary procedures in Michigan from fiscal year 1974 to fiscal year 1978 was a significant factor that influenced the decision of the director of BSS to adopt a modified ZBB format at the beginning of the 1978-79 budget cycle. Three aspects of this drift toward ZBB are significant: the gradual decentralization of budgetary decision making; the requirement that alternative levels of funding (and the implications of those alternatives) be prepared by operating units at the beginning of the budget cycle rather than the more traditional budget request; and the requirement that more analytic justifications accompany budget submissions. This pattern of change is described below.

Program budgeting was adopted with the 1973-74 Executive Budget. In typical program-budgeting fashion, the 1973-74 Executive Budget was organized by major program area rather than by department; nevertheless, an elaborate crosswalk to department budgets was included, partly as a response to legislative resistance to the program format. While program budgeting in Michigan has generally been viewed as a failure, as evidenced by the steady erosion of the program-budgeting format in the Executive Budget from 1973-74 to 1976-77, some aspects of program budgeting (such as needs assessment and measurement of budgetary impacts remained; the more visible (and politically disruptive) aspects of program budgeting were scrapped.

Economic forecasts projecting a grim fiscal climate for fiscal year 1976-77 stimulated another budgetary innovation, which was called target budgeting. Departments were required to submit 1976-77 budget requests at the target levels of 92 percent and 97 percent of the previous year's (1975-76) appropriations. The format included measures of need or demand, and of the output and impact relative to those needs or demands that could be achieved with 3 percent or 8 percent reductions from previous program levels.

Target budgeting required departments, and divisions within departments, to establish priorities and determine how a reduction of 3 percent or 8 percent could be achieved, presumably with minimal impact on clients, recipients, and essential services. Various departments reacted differently to target budgeting; some proposed large reductions in a few programs, while others required each unit or division to propose reductions of the target amounts. The ensuing documents were called target budget management plans, implying that they proposed how the department would manage if the target reduction were made. The Department of Management and Budget (DMB) prepared the governor's Executive Budget for FY 1976-77 from these management plans. Most departmental budgets were lower than the previous year's, some by less than 3 percent, others by more than 8 percent. (Notable exceptions were the Departments of Social Services and Corrections. Although many individual programs within Social Services were reduced, the required increases in AFDC [Aid to Families with Dependent Children] Medicaid, and other public assistance programs pushed the department total higher than the previous year's.)

Target budgeting continued into FY 1977-78 with the establishment of increased target levels of 95 percent, 100 percent, and 108 percent of the FY 1976-77 appropriations. These percentages remained the same for the FY 1978-79 management plans. The requirement that departments provide quantifiable measures of need or demand for services (a legacy from program budgeting), of output possible at each target-resource level, and of the impact of operating at that level was continued, which, in effect, suggests that the earlier PPB experiment and target budgeting were merged. This merger of budgetary procedures allowed the Department of Social Services to reject the idea that needs could be realistically presented in a management plan that only allowed budgetary reductions in FY 1976-77. Instead, the department submitted an X percent budget with a varying percentage above the target levels, which presumably reflected an assessment of programmatic needs as defined by the department. A similar level was added above the 108 percent top target for FY 1977-78; this was euphemistically called the continuation level. In FY 1978-79 it was called the zero-base budget request (ZBBR) level. While not soliciting this response to target budgeting, by FY 1978-79 the Management and Budget staff reviewing the departmental management plans had accepted the approach as representative of the department's program proposals and needs.

Two events occurred in BSS to set the stage for the adoption of a modified ZBB procedure in FY 1978-79. First, a reorganization of BSS had been completed just prior to the beginning of the 1978-79 budget cycle. Second, BSS had a new director who had been in the post

nine months prior to the beginning of the 1978-79 cycle. Two principal concerns guided his interest in zero-base budgeting: he wanted
to use the budget as a tool to set new management priorities; and he
felt that the need-level requests of BSS had not received favorable
treatment in recent years, resulting in unacceptable program reductions in several areas. ZBB was evaluated as a procedure that would
strengthen the management function of budgeting. [8] Moreover, similarities between the target-budgeting approach required by the Department of Management and Budget, and ZBB suggested that it would be
feasible to convert the target approach to ZBB for internal budgetary
decision making in BSS. The director of BSS later requested the department budget staff to assist him in developing a ZBB process designed so that his bureau could develop the FY 1978-79 target budget
management plan. The cooperative relationship between the central
budget staff and BSS perhaps made implementation of ZBB easier
than one would ordinarily expect. More typically, an agency finds itself in an adversary relationship with a central budget staff.

IMPLEMENTATION OF ZBB

    A conclusion that seems to reappear in the growing public-policy
literature on implementation is that centralized decisions divorced
from local needs generally lead to policy failure. In budgeting this is
also illustrated by the experience with PPB at the federal level. Resistance from below is bound to develop when budgetary roles and
routines are radically altered; consequently, one natural implementation strategy is to gradually change procedures over more than one
fiscal year. In the case of zero-base budgeting in BSS, this strategy
was adopted because of both the broader budgetary environment
sketched above and specific implementation decisions within BSS.
    In adapting ZBB to the bureau's needs, several crucial deci-
sions were made. First, the previous practice of across-the-board
reductions to bring budgets below the FY 1977-78 target level of 95
percent would be maintained. This eliminated the aspect of ZBB that
compares each part of the appropriations base of established programs to each proposed increase or new program. The threatening
aspects of this comparison were thus eliminated. This decision was
to hold only for the first year of the implementation, however. In the
second year (FY 1979-80) there would be no protection of the base,
and no across-the-board provisions regarding the 95 percent level.
    A second modification occurred in the level of staff involvement
in the ZBB process. Because of time constraints (as stated, the budget process was already underway), staff at the operating level of
programs (county offices) were not involved. Only central office staff

(with a few exceptions) participated in the process, though all program units in BSS took part in the ZBB exercise.

Third, special decision packages for ZBB were not prepared. Two reasons dictated this decision. First, since FY 1978-79 was, in a sense, a trial year for ZBB, only program increases and new programs were compared. While this is obviously a substantial modification of the original ZBB procedure,[9] the decision can be justified on the grounds that, since the BSS budget is, to a great extent, uncontrollable, it would be unrealistic to actually rank all decision packages if over 80 percent of the budget cannot really be altered in a given fiscal year. Moreover, focusing only on program increases and new programs has the advantage of familiarizing program units with the ranking process of ZBB without posing initial threats and thereby generating the resistance that is so characteristic of budget reforms.

A second reason why decision packages were not prepared is related to the broader budgetary environment. Since ZBB was adopted primarily for internal management, it was apparent that budget decisions at the BSS level would have to be crosswalked into the target-budgeting format used by all other state agencies. This problem was avoided by using an existing procedure called a program-revision request (PRR), which was the basis for initial budget submissions. By adapting the ZBB experiment to existing procedure, BSS avoided the paperwork bottlenecks that characterized PPB, and also seem to provoke criticism of zero-base budgeting elsewhere. Also, staff-training time was reduced and, again, anticipated resistance to ZBB was minimized by building on existing and familiar procedure.

PRRs were ranked in priority order by each program office director and submitted to the BSS director. The BSS director then established his priorities for ranking PRRs. He decided upon four priority levels, for program increases, and ranked these as follows: (1) the minimum level required to meet costs of mandated services; (2) staffing to maintain current service levels or to address most urgent expansion needs; (3) staffing to improve worker/client ratios and for program expansion of second priority; (4) staff to further improve caseload ratios and for third-priority expansion requests. The three priorities for expansion were determined largely by judgments of the BSS director and the office directors in a series of meetings; however, final ranking was done by the BSS director.

The next stage of the 1978-79 budget cycle occurred at the department level. BSS submitted the ZBB budget request, with the four priority levels, to the director of the department, thereby allowing him to participate in the ZBB exercise by reranking the program increases to come to final decisions before submission to Management and Budget. In previous years when the X percent or continuation-level request was too high for him to accept, he had often arbitrarily reduced a bureau's request by a sufficient percentage to make the request acceptable to Management and Budget. While this still occurred in several bureaus, the BSS 1978-79 request, which established priorities, fared much better. The department director accepted priorities 1 and 2, which meant, in effect, that he accepted the judgment of the director of BSS. He then ranked and accepted or rejected priority-3 and -4 programs.

The internal process ended with the consolidation of the BSS management plan into the required DMB format. Targets of 95 percent and 100 percent had been the base continually, and remained the same. The first priority level of the ZBB ranking became the 108 percent budget (it has slightly more than 8 percent over the previous year's appropriation levels). The second priority level, and those programs accepted by the director from the third and fourth levels, were combined to form the ZBBR-level target of the department's management plan. This totaled a cumulative increase of approximately 20 percent over the previous year's appropriation. A ranked list of departmental priorities for BSS at the 108 percent and ZBBR levels was provided to Management and Budget, reflecting the integration of the modified ZBB exercise with the target-budgeting approach used by all state departments in Michigan.

The drift of BSS toward zero-base budgeting can be traced to 1975 and 1976 when there was no independent BSS budget request, reflecting department dominance of the budget process prior to submission to the Department of Management and Budget. This legacy of program budgeting began to change with the use of target budgeting from 1977 to 1979. While there was more involvement of BSS in the budgetary decision making at the beginning of the budget cycle, the experience in FY 1977-78 was instrumental in the decision to adopt a modified ZBB procedure for FY 1978-79. In particular, the department director did not accept the target levels proposed by BSS. Due to budgetary needs in other parts of the department and a tightening of federal funds supporting BSS programs, the director reduced the department budget request at the 108 percent target level to $161.9 million—$500,000 more than the BSS request at the 100 percent target level. While the continuation level was allowed to stand, it was not vigorously defended when the department budget was reviewed by the Department of Management and Budget. The 1977-78 Executive Budget totaled $163.4 million, a 12.9 percent reduction from the BSS continuation request. This amounted to 101 percent of the base, resulting in little or no increases in some programs and requiring reductions in others. The lesson of FY 1977-78, from the BSS standpoint, was that although target budgeting increased bureau involvement in the budget process, it did not ensure that BSS priorities would remain intact, since they were not explicitly presented in the target format. This, plus the acceptance of the low level in the BSS request for FY 1977-78, prompted the director of BSS to use a zero-base budgeting approach in FY 1978-79.

THE IMPACT OF ZBB: A
PRELIMINARY ASSESSMENT

We are cautious in attributing changes in the BSS budget for FY 1978-79 to the ZBB procedure. For example, the economic conditions in Michigan have a major impact on the budgetary support bureaus and departments receive, as noted in the Executive Budget. In the case of the Department of Social Services, there was an 11 percent increase in 1976-77, a 9 percent increase in 1977-78, and only a 1 percent increase in 1978-79. BSS, in contrast, received a 6.5 percent increase in 1978-79. It would be inaccurate, however, to attribute the relative success of BSS to the zero-base process. Since two major portions of the department's budget—public assistance and Medicaid—respond (in a countercyclical way) to the economic climate, the improved Michigan economy produced automatic reductions in public assistance grants and Medicaid. Therefore, a direct comparison between BSS and other parts of the department is not strictly valid even though BSS did improve its budgetary position from 1977-78 to 1978-79. Furthermore, the 6.5 percent increase above the 100 percent base in FY 1978-79 is close to the mean increase for all departments in the state. In short, ZBB may have made a difference in the total BSS budget, but aggregate comparisons do not tell the full story.

A more effective way to gauge the impact of a budget reform like the modified ZBB procedure described in this case study is to determine if it had an effect on management decision making. This can be seen, in part, by comparing the percentage increases over the base for the units in BSS, as illustrated in Table 5.1. All of the appropriations units in BSS (with the exception of Social Services Administration, which is not comparable to the other units) are listed. Comparing FY 1978-79 to 1977-78, a Spearman's coefficient of rank-order correlation, of -.084, suggests that a change in management priorities were reflected in the budget. This can be further illustrated by contrasting two units: one that did poorly under the new ZBB procedures, and one that improved its budgetary position.

Protective Services for Children had, for several years, received favorable budgetary treatment. Notice that in 1976-77 it was the only unit in BSS to receive an increase over the base. In 1977-78 the unit received the largest percentage increase. This pattern, and the continuing judgment of the unit's manager that the unit is essential

TABLE 5.1

Appropriations Units within the Bureau of Social Services

Appropriations Unit	Percentage Increase above the Appropriations Base		
	1976-77	1977-78	1978-79
Community Placement for Adults	(5.57)	9.3	25.0
Community Placement for Children[a]	n.a.	0.3	1.3
Day Care[b]	n.a.	0.0	1.5
Delinquency Prevention[c]	n.a.	(0.6)	10.6
Employment and Training	(12.8)	0.5	7.4
Basic Social Services	(2.5)	(0.3)	12.7
Institutional Services Division	(11.0)	5.0	0.0
Protective Services for Adults[d]	n.a.	0.5	9.8
Protective Services for Children	8.2	27.8	0.0
Rehabilitation of the Blind	(1.8)	8.6	15.0

[a]Created in 1977-78 from Basic Social Services and Institutional Services.

[b]Created by splitting Day Care and Employment and Training.

[c]Created from Basic Services, Employment and Training, and Protective Services for Children.

[d]Created from Basic Social Services.

Note: Percentages in parentheses are negative; n. a. indicates data not applicable.

Source: Departmental data.

and not really subject to scrutiny, led the manager to comply with the
ZBB process requirements only minimally. The basic justifications
for the requested staff increase of 175 persons and requested additional services—at a cost of $5.3 million—were that this is a high-
priority program and that these services tend to prevent delinquent
behavior in the same children later. With no documentation and no
further justification, this was considered one of the weaker ZBB presentations in BSS. Under ZBB, the Protective Services program did
not fare well either within or outside BSS. No increase was provided
at the priority-1 level; and staff increase of 65 persons ($1.2 million)
was accepted at the priority-2 level. Further increases were provided
at levels 3 and 4, thereby including the $5.3 million request at level
4. The department request included only level 2 (as part of the ZBBR
target level); no increase was provided at the 108 percent level. The
Executive Budget showed the 108 percent level (no increase).

In contrast, the Basic Social Services unit, consisting of counseling and casework services for adults and families, had received
no increases over the past two years. The unit's caseload had been
increasing in that time, so its relative worker/client ratio was de-
teriorating. Looking at its budget from a ZBB standpoint enabled it
to escape the paralysis it had felt in past years because its program
was so large ($57.5 million; a staff of 1,200). There was difficulty
in explaining precisely how much of the money and staff for each component of the program was used. The ZBB process forced the unit to
look at each component and to set priorities; the large program then
became more manageable and, as a result, the request more fully
documented the need for additional staff and resources. Under ZBB,
the bureau request for this program was increased $13 million at the
priority-1 level (23 percent), with increases requested at each subsequent level up to the priority-4 level, where the request was for a
$26 million increase (45 percent). The Executive Budget accepted an
increase of $7.3 million, or 12.7 percent.

While other factors may have produced these results, the effect
of required priority setting under ZBB, both in BSS and at the department level, cannot be discounted. ZBB allowed the directors of BSS
and the department to compare one program, large and ill defined,
with a second program, well defined and supported as a whole with
little analytical documentation. Breaking down the components of the
Protective Services program showed that some parts were not as essential as some parts of Basic Social Services. This was a new experience for managers of both programs as well as for the BSS director and the department director. It should be remembered that
the nature of most of the service programs in BSS is such that all
program managers believe that their programs are essential to the
well-being of clients. Forced priority setting means admitting one

program is more important than another; while perhaps painful, this has been constructive both for budget preparation and, more importantly, for management.

CONCLUSIONS

Our case study of ZBB in the Bureau of Social Services of the state of Michigan suggests the following conclusions.

To begin with, the budgetary environment in the state facilitated the adoption of ZBB by the bureau in fiscal year 1978-79. Specifically, the budget process experienced several changes in format and procedure over the five-year period (1975-79). As a result of these changes, it is most appropriate to describe the shifts in procedure as an evolution of budget format rather than as the radical departures from routine that have characterized reform efforts elsewhere. While these changes certainly produced some grumbling in the bureaucracy, they also introduced program managers and bureau heads to different budget concepts, formats, and procedures. The obvious advantage of an evolutionary process is that something like ZBB is not treated as a completely alien concept. On the contrary, as the case study illustrated, it was not very difficult to merge target budgeting with ZBB. As a result, the BSS version of ZBB did not resemble the "pure" model as outlined by Peter Phyrr. [10]

Proponents of ZBB argue that the various components of the process must be accommodated to specific budgetary environments. The case study of ZBB in the Bureau of Social Services shows how this occurs in practice. Specifically, to ease the transition from target budgeting to ZBB, the bureau head decided that the base (1977-78 appropriations) would represent the lowest level of funding in the 1978-79 ZBB budget request. While this departs quite a bit from the basic ZBB model, it undoubtedly facilitated acceptance of the process within BSS and thereby increased the probability that it would be successfully implemented. It is anticipated that in the next budget cycle (fiscal year 1979-80), the base will not receive the same protection that it did in 1978-79. If this decision occurs it will represent one further evolution in budgetary procedure.

Despite the qualified success of the ZBB exercise, it is worth noting two obstacles that affect the success of the process. The first is related to the characteristics of the BSS budget that reduce the possibility of significant changes in program funding levels and broad shifts in program priorities. It has been pointed out that, at the federal level, for example, it is unrealistic to subject uncontrollable budgets to a zero-base review. While the concept of uncontrollability is not used at the state level, it nevertheless applies in this case.

Therefore, even if the base is not protected in the 1979-80 budget cycle, probably no more than 20 percent of the bureau's budget could be affected by a ZBB exercise. If this happens it would mirror the experience of most federal departments during the 1979 fiscal year, when President Carter's first budget was prepared according to ZBB procedures. [11]

A second obstacle is really subsumed under the politics and economics of the budget cycle. In brief, even if budgetary decisions reflect ZBB priorities within the bureau and even the department, there is no guarantee that these decisions will stand when the ZBB format is crosswalked at the Management and Budget review stage. This is not a shortcoming of ZBB, but rather reflects the political and economic realities of budgeting at the state level. Furthermore, the case study makes no attempt to anticipate the reaction of ZBB by the legislature. Past research has shown that, at the federal level, the congressional response to reform (in this case PPB) at the appropriations stage was lukewarm at best. [12] In Michigan the legislature has not been receptive to budget reforms in the past. This obstacle is being avoided in fiscal year 1978-79 by simply crosswalking the ZBB format into target budgeting. Nevertheless, the legislature can obviously undo ZBB decisions during the appropriations phase.

Our final comment about the case concerns the compatibility of the ZBB exercise with the traditional incremental budget process. In a National Journal report on the new executive budget process, Jerome A. Miles, director of management and finance of the U.S. Agriculture Department, is quoted as saying, "When you're through with zero-base budgeting, you have the best incremental budgeting system I've ever seen." [13] The case study of ZBB in the Bureau of Social Services supports this conclusion. The BSS director, it should be recalled, grafted ZBB onto the existing budget process because he viewed it as a tool to support budget expansion. This decision fits the description of bureau strategy that seems to be the linchpin of incremental budgeting. Furthermore, while ZBB did require more rigorous justification of budget requests, and sharpened some of the debate over budget priorities, the process did not alter traditional budgetary roles. On the contrary, it is often said that one of the most effective ways to argue for an increase in one's budget is to point out the dire effects of a budget cut. ZBB fits this tactic rather well.

Reform zealots would probably be unhappy with this conclusion. Yet if modest improvements in the budget process are what one expects (and this, we feel, is the most realistic position to hold), then the skeptics of reform should perhaps rethink their position. The case study of budget reform in the Michigan Bureau of Social Services is a start in that direction.

NOTES

1. Allen Schick, "A Death in the Bureaucracy: The Demise of Federal PPB," Public Administration Review 33 (March/April, 1973): 146-49.

2. Edwin L. Harper, Fred A. Kramer, and Andrew M. Rouse, "Implementation and Use of PBB in Sixteen Federal Agencies," Public Administration Review 29 (December 1969): 626.

3. Aaron Wildavsky, Budgeting (Boston: Little, Brown, 1975), p. 356.

4. Robert N. Anthony, "Zero-Base Budgeting is a Fraud," The Wall Street Journal, April 27, 1977, p. 22.

5. Robert W. Hartman, "Next Steps in Budget Reform: Zero-Base Review and the Budgetary Process," Policy Analysis 3 (Summer 1977): 389.

6. Joel Havemann, "The Budget—A Tax Cut, Little Else," National Journal 10 (January 28, 1978): 129.

7. Allen Schick, "Budget Gap," Public Administration Review 37 (September/October 1977): 534.

8. See Allen Schick, "The Road to PPB: The Stages of Budget Reform," Public Administration Review 26 (December 1966): 243-58.

9. Peter Phyrr, "The Zero-Base Approach to Government Budgeting," Public Administration Review 37 (January/February 1977): 1-8.

10. Ibid.

11. Havemann, op. cit., p. 129.

12. James E. Jernberg, "Information Change and Congressional Behavior: A Caveat for PPB Reformers," Journal of Politics 33 (August 1969): 722-40.

13. Havemann, op. cit., p. 129.

6

ZERO-BASE BUDGETING: THE SOUTH DAKOTA EXPERIENCE

Donald C. Dahlin

This study discusses the South Dakota government's experiment with zero-base budgeting (ZBB), as reflected in the experience of its Department of Public Safety. * Because the ZBB experiment was con-

---

*Besides the Department of Public Safety, the Department of Environmental Protection, the Bureau of Finance and Management, the Office of the Attorney General, and the legislature were involved in the experiment. Nonetheless, because my personal involvement in the project was as secretary of the Department of Public Safety, this discussion, of necessity, reflects the perceptions of ZBB seen from the Public Safety perspective. Unquestionably, serving as secretary heightened my perception of ZBB in many respects. No doubt, as well, occupying this position put blinders on my vision in other ways. In an effort both to confirm what I saw and to correct what I might have missed or seen incorrectly, this discussion was reviewed by other actors in the process. Their comments were helpful and have been incorporated. Nonetheless, I bear final responsibility for the chapter, and the overall vantage point from which the experiment is viewed is still primarily that of the Department of Public Safety.

Donald C. Dahlin is chairperson of the Political Science Department and director of the Criminal Justice Studies Program at the University of South Dakota. Formerly, he served as the Secretary of Public Safety in South Dakota.

ceived and approved by a strongly Republican legislature, to be used primarily by agencies of a Democratic executive branch, it is important to first understand, in general terms, the governmental structure of South Dakota as well as the political context in which ZBB was conducted in the state. Against this background, the actual implementation of ZBB is examined. Finally, based upon the South Dakota experience, an effort is made to draw conclusions and to make recommendations about ZBB that have more general applicability.

BACKGROUND: THE SOUTH DAKOTA GOVERNMENTAL STRUCTURE

Like most state governments, the South Dakota executive branch consists of agencies under the jurisdiction not only of the governor but of other elected officials as well, including the attorney general, the secretary of state, the state treasurer, the state auditor, the commissioner of school and public lands, and the public utility commissioners. Gubernatorially appointed boards and commissions such as the Board of Regents, the Board of Charities and Corrections, and the Board of Transportation further serve to fragment executive power in the state. Nonetheless, as a result of a constitutional amendment approved in the 1972 election, the governor's authority over most executive-branch agencies has been enhanced considerably.

Agencies under the governor's control are organized into a cabinet form of government consisting of 16 line agencies headed by secretaries appointed by the governor and confirmed by the Senate, and four staff agencies headed by gubernatorially appointed commissioners. The staff agency with principal responsibility for assisting the governor in the preparation of his budget is the Bureau of Finance and Management. Since 1973, a program-budgeting system has been used by the governor in preparing his budgets for presentation to the legislature. [1] For its part, the South Dakota legislature consists of a 35-member Senate and a 70-member House of Representatives. Members of both houses are elected to two-year terms. Annual sessions run for 45 days in odd-numbered years and 30 days in even-numbered years. Professional-staff services are provided to the legislature through the Legislative Research Council and the Auditor General's Office.

To facilitate consideration of the governor's budget, the legislature uses a Joint Appropriations Committee consisting currently of 20 members. The commission is cochaired by a member from the House and one from the Senate. To ensure more in-depth review of agency requests, the committee divides itself into two subcommittees, each headed by one of the cochairmen. Using the governor's budget recommendations as the base, it is these subcommittees which play the major role in setting agency budget levels.

The involvement of the rest of the legislature in the budget process is ordinarily rather small (a fact which causes some resentment among other legislators). Normally, the Joint Appropriations Bill does not arrive on the floor of either house until the last day or two of the session. As a practical matter, the full legislature has little choice but to approve the bill as presented, and approval of the bill as presented is the normal outcome.

THE POLITICAL CONTEXT OF ZBB IN SOUTH DAKOTA

Against this general background, the politics of ZBB in South Dakota can be examined. This examination should begin with the last day of the 1976 legislative session. True to form, the General Appropriations Bill for fiscal year (FY) 1977 had arrived on the floor of the legislature on the final day of the legislature session. After an hour or two of discussion, the bill passed the Democratic-controlled Senate (19 Democrats as compared to 16 Republicans) by a comfortable 24–7 vote (four members did not vote). The bill was then sent to the Republican-controlled House (37 Republicans as compared to 33 Democrats). In the House, Majority Leader Walter Dale Miller proposed to amend the General Appropriations Bill by cutting the general funded agencies of state government, across the board, by 2.1 percent. In turn, the money saved would be used to increase state aid to elementary and secondary education at the local level. Representative Miller's motion prevailed on a nearly straight party-line vote, and the longest legislative day in the history of the state began. After several efforts at compromise throughout Friday night, Saturday, and Saturday night, the bill, as originally proposed, was adopted by both houses on Sunday.

Although failing to achieve the immediate objective of cutting the budget, this action (coupled with vigorous opposition to any form of income tax) set the Republican cut-big-government theme for the 1976 legislative election. (Having been elected to a four-year term in 1974, the governor was not up for reelection). When the ballots were counted on November 2, 1976, the Republican party had won an overwhelming victory, gaining control of the House by a 48-to-22 margin and the Senate by a 24-to-11 margin.

In light of this enormous victory, at least in part won on a cut-government theme, it should not come as a surprise to learn that the first bill (HB 501) introduced into the House of Representatives in the 1977 session was a bill to establish zero-base budgeting on a pilot basis. It also should come as no surprise to learn that the bill's seven sponsors represented the Republican legislative leadership of both the House and Senate. Interestingly enough, however, the sponsors did not include any members of the Joint Appropriations Committee.

As introduced, HB 501 was eight pages in length. The bill called for the creation of a special legislative committee to study the ZBB concept during the 1977 adjournment period and, according to Section 2 of the bill, "report its findings on the feasibility of implementing the zero-base budget concept in subsequent years to the 1978 legislature in the form of a report and one or more bills as deemed necessary." The Commerce and Consumer Affairs, and Environmental Protection Departments were the agencies named to prepare a zero-base budget during the pilot period.

In some detail, the remainder of the bill set out definitions, procedures, and timetables to be followed in using the zero-base approach. One final point regarding the bill: Most bills passed by the legislature go into effect on July 1 of the year in which they are passed. However, a bill can go into effect immediately upon its signing by the governor if the measure contains an emergency clause asserting that because the act is "necessary for the support of the state government and its existing public institutions, an emergency is hereby declared to exist, and this Act shall be in full force and effect from and after its passage and approval."* Bills with an emergency clause require a two-thirds vote of the members-elect of each house in order to pass. HB 501 contained an emergency clause because the timetables established in the bill presumed implementation prior to July 1, 1977.

HB 501 was referred to the House State Affairs Committee for consideration. The chairman of the House State Affairs Committee was Representative Miller, majority leader of the House and prime sponsor of HB 501. As members of the Kneip administration discussed the proposal, no clear and detailed strategy emerged. Program budgeting was an innovation of the Administration. Having made that change in the state's budgeting system, a further change to zero-base budgeting was never seriously considered. At the same time, in a specific reaction to HB 501, members of the administration did voice considerable concern about the potential workload that might result from ZBB and about the political uses to which ZBB might be put.

---

*This is boiler-plate language, used on all emergency bills. So far as I know, there are no objective criteria to determine whether, in fact, an emergency exists; apparently, if two-thirds of the members-elect of both houses agree, the matter at issue, by definition, is of an emergency nature.

However, the political appeal of ZBB was also recognized. The net result was a rather low-key administration response to HB 501.

The secretary of environmental protection, Allyn Lockner, did appear in opposition to the bill, but his opposition was limited to the workload impact of ZBB on his relatively small agency (FY 1978 budget of $1.15 million, with 51.5 full-time equivalent [FTE] employees). Beyond this limited opposition, Henry J. Decker, commissioner of the Bureau of Finance and Management, testified not in opposition to the concept of ZBB, but in opposition to some features of the concept embodied in HB 501. As an example, Commissioner Decker voiced some opposition to the selection of the Department of Commerce and Consumer Affairs and the Department of Environmental Protection to prepare the zero-base budget. In their place, he recommended using the Department of Natural Resources, as an example of a small but rapidly growing department, and the Department of Social Services, as an example of a large, complex department. Commissioner Decker also expressed concern about the use of the activity level as the starting point in building a zero-base budget. Commissioner Decker pointed out that the South Dakota state government currently appropriated and budgeted at the program, rather than activity, level and suggested that moving to the activity level would create enormous workload problems.

The commissioner also expressed a desire to make the bill more compatible with the state's accounting system so as to maximize the opportunities to use existing data in developing a ZBB budget. At the conclusion of comments such as these, Commissioner Decker presented to the committee a list of 29 proposed changes. In response, the committee did not adopt Commissioner Decker's suggested changes, but, instead, adopted a series of clarifying amendments proposed by Hal Wick, a freshman legislator from the Sioux Falls area who had developed a great personal interest in the ZBB approach. These amendments also removed the name of the Department of Commerce and Consumer Affairs from the bill and substituted in its place the Department of Public Safety and the Attorney General's Office.

With these amendments, the bill was sent to the floor with a "Do pass" recommendation from the committee, on a straight party-line vote. The bill as amended in committee passed on the House floor, with 60 votes for the bill, 7 against, and three members not voting. When the bill arrived in the Senate, it was referred to the Senate State Affairs Committee. At this point, the Republican attorney general, William Janklow, who had volunteered his agency to participate in the pilot project, decided he did not wish to have to take direction from the governor's Bureau of Finance and Management. Accordingly, amendments were adopted allowing him to devise his own budget forms and otherwise proceed independently of Public Safety,

Environmental Protection, and the Bureau of Finance and Management in the preparation of a zero-base budget.

The bill, with these amendments, passed the Senate by a vote of 29 to 3, with three members not voting. Subsequently, the House concurred with the Senate's amendments and the bill was signed into law by Governor Kneip on April 1, 1977.

Analysis of these events that led to the adoption of zero-base budgeting in South Dakota might well have caused a detached observer to anticipate implementation problems with ZBB for at least three reasons. First, those responsible for implementing ZBB were not the ones responsible for passing the ZBB proposal. Clearly, HB 501 was not the creature of the Kneip administration and the executive branch. Instead, this was entirely a legislative initiative. However, as a legislative idea, the proposal was not sponsored by a single member of the Joint Appropriations Committee, which logically would have to implement the pilot project and evaluate its utility as a decision-making tool in the appropriations process.

Second, the fact that the bill was introduced as the first House bill of the 1977 session by the entire Republican leadership of the House and Senate, to be tested by (or on) two executive-branch agencies under the control of a Democratic governor, inevitably fostered a climate of suspicion rather than one of trust. The very fact that the bill was written in such detail undoubtedly reflected the sponsors' fear that, without considerable specificity, the executive agencies might somehow avoid giving ZBB a fair test. At the same time, the affected administrative agencies were very suspicious of the political uses to which ZBB might be put and, as a consequence, were bound to scrutinize the bill with extreme care in an effort to prevent political capital from being made out of the project.

Third, the popular political appeal of ZBB, coupled with the political partisanship necessarily involved when one branch of government, controlled by one party, attempts to place requirements on agencies of another branch of government, controlled by another party, meant that the bill, while quite detailed, was never carefully examined with a view toward minimizing implementation problems for the affected agencies.

IMPLEMENTING ZERO-BASE BUDGETING

As finally passed, HB 501 set up some very strict timetables. Specifically, the law required that on or before June 15, 1977, both the attorney general and the Bureau of Finance and Management would have to prepare suitable forms to accomplish the project. Since the legislative committee charged with overseeing the zero-base experiment was to have not less than 15 days to review and comment on the forms prior to their final issuance, the forms in fact had to be ready on or before June 1. The affected agencies had until August 1, 1977 to prepare their actual FY 1979 budget request in a ZBB format. The legislative committee then had until August 15, 1977 to comment on the initial submission. If necessary, new forms would then be issued and the agencies would resubmit another zero-base request by no later than September 20, 1977.

Given these stringent deadlines, initial implementation efforts were concentrated in two directions. First, there was a considerable effort made to understand the literature of ZBB and the experience of other states. Conveniently enough, the January-February 1977 issue of the Public Administration Review contained an article by Peter Phyrr on ZBB, and this article was carefully examined and discussed within the Department of Public Safety and also with officials in the Bureau of Finance and Management. [2] Phyrr's book on ZBB was also read, and pertinent excerpts of it were distributed to division directors and fiscal personnel in the Department of Public Safety. [3] Officials in the Georgia Department of Public Safety were contacted by phone, on the notion that their experience with ZBB might be especially relevant. They were kind enough to furnish their zero-base request for FY 1978.

As a final (and, to some extent, perhaps desperate) effort to discover the magic key that would allow a ZBB request to be turned out with ease and sophistication, the South Dakota Public Safety Department sent 34 people (essentially all program managers, division directors, and fiscal personnel in the department) to a two-day training session offered in Pierre by Executive Management Service Inc. of Arlington, Virginia. Executive Management's course had been developed to assist federal officials attempting to prepare their budgets using the ZBB format, and so it was not completely germane to the South Dakota situation. Nonetheless, it was helpful.

In addition to reviewing the literature of ZBB and the experience of selected other states in implementing ZBB, early implementation efforts in South Dakota moved in a second direction, toward careful review of HB 501 as finally passed. In attempting to identify questions, problems, and issues of the ZBB law, the Department of Public Safety and the Department of Environmental Protection worked very closely with the Bureau of Finance and Management. Informal contacts occurred both prior to and immediately after passage of HB 501. More formally, on April 19, 1977 and again on April 21, 1977, the secretaries of the two departments plus personnel from the Bureau of Finance and Management, including the commissioner, met in an effort to identify questions regarding the law as well as to suggest possible answers to those questions.

As a result of these contacts, several concerns were identified, of which two were major in significance. The first major concern had previously been identified by Commissioner Decker in his testimony to the House State Affairs Committee; this concern was over the use of the activity level as the starting point in the ZBB process.

Initially, the problem was simple to determine what an activity was. As defined in Section 1, subsection 8, of the law, an activity consisted of "operational functions employed to carry out a program which can be measured by workload measures which illustrate how the activity is being performed." Clearly, an activity was a subunit of a program, but how these subunits were to be identified was much less clear. Thus, for example, within the Law Enforcement Program of the Division of Highway Patrol, the work time of individual patrolmen is catalogued in over 100 different ways. Each of these could be viewed as an activity, as defined above. Patently, however, to use such a detailed unit as the foundation for the preparation of decision packages would entail an incredible (and, given the timetable, impossible) workload. Similarly, the Department of Environmental Protection had subdivided their Water Hygiene Program into 52 separate missions, which also could be viewed as activities. No doubt, the major reason why the two departments were having such difficulty defining "activity" was the fact that the formal use of activities was not a part of South Dakota's budget system.

Given the relative size and sophistication of the South Dakota state government, decision makers had never before felt a routine need to appropriate and budget on an activity basis. Consequently, if used at all, subprogram elements (other than traditional budget-line items such as travel, and contractual services) were used on a selective, nonbudget basis to track costs by geographical area (for example, a district patrol office, or a driver-license exam station) or to keep track of time spent on various functions. This fact meant that, even if an agreed-upon definition of "activity" could be reached, there was no assurance that accurate and adequate workload and/or budgetary data would be available for use in building a solid zero-base budget. To the contrary, the presumption had to be that sufficient data at the activity level were not available and, hence, zero-base budgets that started at that level would very likely be inaccurate, unreliable, and, hence, useless as budget documents.

In short, starting ZBB in South Dakota at the activity level would require an incredible amount of effort, which unfortunately would very likely result in a poor product that in turn would undoubtedly be criticized by the legislature. Given this prospect, the concern of the two departments and the Bureau of Finance and Management perhaps can be better appreciated.

The second major concern regarding HB 501 as passed centered on the concept of the decision package. Section 1, subsection 17, defined decision packages as constituting the

> identification of alternative levels of costs and benefits of
> a specific activity, program, office, division, department
> and department group in a manner that allows each succes-
> sive level of management and the legislature to rank the
> priority of and evaluate the necessity of [each] activity,
> program, office, division, department or department
> group against other activities, programs, offices, divi-
> sions, departments, and department groups; such ranking
> and evaluation to include but not be limited to examination
> of the missions, objectives, and goals, and consequences
> of effecting or not effecting the same, and the examination
> of alternatives to each activity, program, office, depart-
> ment or department group including costs and benefits.

In examining this definition, it appeared that separate decision packages might have to be developed first at the activity level; then again at the program level; then again at the office level; then again at the division level; then again at the department level; and, finally, at the department-group level. *

This interpretation received strength from Section 7 of the act, which required that each agency "prepare a decision package or series of decision packages for each activity, program, office, division, department, and department group." Section 7 went on to provide that the minimum funding level of each decision package would be no more "than sixty percent of the fiscal year 1978 budgeted level for an activity, seventy-five percent of the fiscal year 1978 budgeted level for a program, eighty percent of the fiscal year 1978 budgeted level for an office or division, eighty-five percent of the fiscal year 1978 budgeted level for a department, and ninety percent of the fiscal year 1978 budgeted level for a departmental group."

---

*The reference to department groups illustrates one of the lesser concerns identified in analyzing the laws. Section 3 of the act defined a department group as comprising the Department of Public Safety and the Attorney General's Office, and yet other sections of the act, notably Sections 4 and 5, provided for separate forms and procedures for the two agencies. Nowhere in the act were these conflicting sections reconciled. For this reason, a zero-base budget at the department-group level was not developed.

If correct, this interpretation of the law's requirements posed two problems. The first problem was the workload such an interpretation would require. Again, under the time constraint noted in the legislation, to prepare well-thought-out and well-documented decision packages at the activity level, or the program level, or the office level, or the division level, or the department level, or the department-group level would be difficult enough. To prepare good decision packages for all of these levels would be impossible.

The second problem posed by the apparent requirement to prepare decision packages at each of these levels was how then to develop a comprehensive ranking of the decision packages so developed. Clearly, it would be possible to rank the decision packages prepared at any one level, but it did not seem possible to rank decision packages prepared at the activity level together with decision packages prepared at the program level, decision packages prepared at the office level, and so on.

Both from a review of the literature and the ZBB course in Pierre, the usual approach appeared to be to use varying funding levels (or decision packages) at a basic decision-unit level and then bring these decision packages forward to reach totals for programs, offices, and so on. [4] Unfortunately, while defining many terms, the act did not define "decision unit," and so there was no ready way to resolve this question of whether or not separate decision packages had to be prepared at every organizational level.

While questions of the act's meaning would have to be finally resolved by the special legislative committee created to oversee the ZBB experiment, the general pressure of the deadlines set forth in the act, and the specific pressure of having to develop a set of forms by June 1, 1977, prompted the Bureau of Finance and Management, in cooperation with the two departments, to make some tentative decisions concerning the practical way to implement HB 501.

First, and foremost, was the decision to use the existing budgetary system to the maximum extent possible in an effort to minimize the workload requirements of all parties, including the legislative committee; for, like the agencies, the committee was familiar with the format of the program-budget system, and the information developed from it. Taking this approach meant that the ZBB requirement for information regarding departmental and division goals, office objectives, program missions, and performance objectives could be adopted whole from the program-budgeting system.

This decision resulted in general acceptance of the program level as the decision unit. This decision reflected Phyrr's approach: that decision units are the "meaningful elements" of an organization and that "each organization must determine for itself what is meaningful." [5] In recommending the program level, the further recommendation was made that the Law Enforcement Program of the Highway Patrol might well benefit from being broken down into five or six activities. This seemed to make sense both because of the size of the program (FY 1978 budget of $4.4 million, with 195 FTE employees) and because the internal information system of the patrol would have the best capacity to provide sufficient and accurate information at this more detailed level.

Finally, the assumption was made that decision packages would be prepared only at the program level (except in the case of the Highway Patrol's Law Enforcement Program, where the activity level would be used), and then would be brought forward to the office, division, and department levels. This approach would comply with the act's requirements that the minimum level of funding at the program level be no more than 75 percent, the minimum level at the office or division level be no more than 80 percent, and so on, because, by definition, the first minimum level would be lower than these other minimum levels.

Having agreed on what seemed to be a practical resolution of some of the problems in the act, the Bureau of Finance and Management proceeded on this basis to draw up the suggested forms and to develop a tentative ZBB Procedures Manual. By using the current budget system to the maximum extent possible, only three new forms had to be developed: (1) a ZBB decision-analysis form, which established the format for providing the required decision-package information for each program (or, in the case of the Law Enforcement Program of the Highway Patrol, for each activity); (2) a ZBB decision-package priority-ranking form, which, as the name suggests, provided the format for comprehensively ranking the individual decision packages; and (3) a ZBB performance-indicator form, which provided for historical performance information for each indicator as well as the work that could be accomplished at the funding levels identified in each of the decision packages.

On May 23, 1977, these proposed forms, along with a letter outlining the problems that the two departments and the bureau saw in the act, were sent to Representative Harold Sieh, chairman of the ZBB Study Committee. Copies of the letter and the forms were also sent to each of the other ZBB Study Committee members. (The study committee consisted of nine members—five senators and four representatives, including six Republicans and three Democrats; and eight Appropriations Committee members and one nonmember, Representative Wick of Sioux Falls.)

Naturally, the two departments also received this same material. In the Department of Public Safety, this material in turn was made available to each of the divisions, along with a request that any comments on the proposed forms be provided to the Secretary's Office by no later than May 31, 1977, so that they could be analyzed and synthesized prior to the first ZBB Study Committee meeting, scheduled for June 10. The comments that came back from the divisions did not indicate any serious problems with the forms, and so, as the June 10 meeting date approached, the big question was whether or not the ZBB Study Committee would accept the approach tentatively taken in regard to the requirements of the act.

The committee began its first meeting at 9:40 a. m. All members except one were in attendance. As background for the meeting, members of the committee had received a ZBB study paper prepared by staff of the Legislative Research Council. The meeting began with Chairman Sieh noting that the committee had been assigned the task to study the "implementation of zero based budgeting using the Office of the Attorney General, Department of Environmental Protection, and Department of Public Safety as pilot agencies. "[6] What followed was a general discussion of zero-base budgeting. This discussion was led by Jim Oliver, of the Texas Legislative Council, who presented the ZBB approach as used by the Texas legislature. This discussion led naturally into a discussion regarding the use of the activity level as the decision unit and the concept of the decision package.

On the activity-level question, after considerable discussion, the committee decided, as a general rule, to allow the agencies to use the program level, rather than the activity level, as the decision unit for the preparation of decision packages. From the discussion, it was clear that the Law Enforcement Program of the Highway Patrol would be the one exception to this general approach.

On the decision-package question, again, after considerable debate, the concept of preparing decision packages only at the lowest (generally, program) level, and then bringing the totals forward to get the final department total, was also accepted.

The committee, having concurred with the general approach taken by the departments and the Bureau of Finance and Management in implementing the act, then easily approved the forms, with only very minor changes.

Shortly after the committee meeting, the decisions reached by the committee were communicated to the Public Safety Department's division directors and fiscal personnel at a staff meeting; and the Bureau of Finance and Management provided the final version of the forms and the ZBB Procedures Manual. The actual preparation of a zero-base budget could now begin.

By the time all of this information was given to the divisions, the end of June was approaching. In order to give the divisions the maximum amount of time to formulate and rank their decision packages, and yet allow time for some review and for preparing the overall ranking, the material was required to be in the Secretary's Office

by July 26, 1977. On this date as well, each division director met
with the secretary and his staff to go over the material that had been
submitted. In turn, on July 27, 1977, the Bureau of Finance and Management held a meeting to go over the material as well. Apart from
general guidance as to procedures and format, the divisions were
given complete freedom to develop the substance of their budget request as they saw fit. Table 6.1 contains summary information about
the ZBB request that resulted from this process

As the table indicates, 94 decision packages were prepared for
31 separate decision units. This produced a total request that was
103.1 percent of the FY 1978 budget, and a request for 467 FTE employees, an increase of 34.1 over the FY 1978 authorization. The
number of decision packages ranged from a low of one for the Juvenile
Justice Delinquency and Prevention Act Program, which was being
phased out, to seven decision packages totaling 511 percent over the
FY 1978 budget for the Motor Carrier Enforcement Program of the
Highway Patrol.

In the normal budget-preparation process, some of the decision
packages would have been cut or deleted altogether in the review carried out at the level of the Office of the Secretary. However, because
of the limited time involved, and because of the experimental nature
of this ZBB project, no effort was made to cut or reduce budget requests. Instead, the review in the Secretary's Office centered on ensuring procedural correctness and overall consistency in the department's submission. Beyond this essentially procedural review, the
primary effort in the Secretary's Office was to prepare the overall
ranking of these 94 decision packages.

Mechanically, this ranking was accomplished through the use
of three-by-five inch cards, each card containing summary information on one decision package. The use of these cards allowed for
tentative rankings to be changed with a minimum of effort. The ranking process took about three hours and involved principally the deputy
secretary and the secretary. In preparing the rankings, decisions had
to be made as to how to handle such essentially technical questions as
the relative priority of administrative decision packages compared
to program-delivery decision packages (program-delivery packages
were ranked ahead of administration packages); and the relative merits
of ranking the first decision package (and hence the first level of funding)—of all programs (or activities) that, it was felt, should be funded—before ranking the second level for any program or activity, or,
as an alternative, ranking together the decision packages necessary
to secure at least an adequate level of funding for programs (or activities) that were felt to be of a priority nature (in practice, the first
option was generally followed).

In addition, the presumption was that a division director's ranking of the decision packages in his division would be accepted unless there were some compelling reason to change rankings. Using this approach, the primary task of the Secretary's Office was to integrate the division directors' rankings into a departmental whole. At the same time, in actual practice, several changes were made in the rankings as they came from the division directors. Had there been more time, these changes, as well as the overall rankings, should have been discussed with the division directors before being submitted to the Bureau of Finance and Management and the ZBB Study Committee. Unfortunately, there was not sufficient time, and so the overall ranking was developed and submitted without the benefit of review and comment by the divisions. One final comment on the ranking process: ranking the top and the bottom groups of decision packages was relatively easy; ranking the large middle group of decision packages was much more difficult.

As the law required, the department's budget was submitted to the Zero-Base Budgeting Study Committee on August 1, 1977. The material was formally reviewed at the committee's second meeting on August 11, 1977. At this meeting, each of the agencies was offered a chance to comment generally on ZBB. In addition selected decision packages were examined to get a feel for the information produced using the ZBB approach. At the conclusion of the meeting, the committee accepted the forms prepared by the Departments of Public Safety and Environmental Protection, with only very minor changes. The attorney general was asked to redo and resubmit some ZBB forms prepared by his office. The committee also voted to direct committee staff to develop legislation to continue ZBB. In drafting this legislation, the staff was further requested to prepare options for the committee's consideration at its final meeting.

THE AFTERMATH OF THE ZERO-BASE
BUDGETING PILOT PROJECT

At this point, then, the ZBB pilot project in South Dakota ended. The aftermath of the project occurred on two fronts. On the first front, the Legislative Research Council did prepare a draft ZBB bill to move ZBB from pilot-project status to being a permanent part of the budget landscape in South Dakota; as requested by the ZBB committee, the bill contained various options to be examined in the process of settling on a final proposal. On October 7, 1977, the ZBB Study Committee held its final meeting to review the staff's work and to reach final agreement on the committee bill to be introduced in the fifty-third session of the legislature.

TABLE 6.1

Decision–Package Data Developed from ZBB Process

Organizational Unit	Decision Unit	Number of Decision Packages Developed	Cumulative Total of Decision Packages as a Percent of FY 1978 Budget
Office of the Secretary	Administration Program	2	97. 6
	Finance and Management Program	3	110. 0
Division of Law Enforcement Assistance Administration	LEAA Administration and Discretionary Grants Program	1	50. 0
	LEAA Grants and Evaluation Program	3	110. 0
	Juvenile Justice and Delinquency Prevention Act Program	1	0. 0
Division of Fire Safety	Protection and Investigation Program	5	140. 0
	Boiler Inspection Program	4	140. 0
	Fire Service Training Program	4	122. 0
Division of Highway Patrol	Law Enforcement Program		
	Field Operations Program	5	124. 0
	Training (activity)	3	105. 0
	Administration (activity)	3	105. 0
	Safety (activity)	3	104. 0

Chemical tests (activity)	4	199.0
Aircraft (activity)	5	142.0
Governor's security (activity)	2	(new)
Motor Vehicle Inspection Program	4	259.0
Motor Carrier Enforcement Program	7	511.0
Division of Motor Vehicles		
Administration Program	2	98.0
Titles and Registration Program	2	75.0
Dealer Inspection Program	3	110.0
Proration and Reciprocity Program	1	59.0
Compensation Program	1	58.0
Ports of Entry Program	2	82.0
Division of Highway Safety		
Administration Program	3	136.0
Driver License Examination Program	3	108.0
Driver License Issuance Program	2	89.0
Driver Improvement Program	4	118.0
Accident Records	3	109.0
Public Information and Education	3	110.0
State and Community Programs	4	110.0
State and Community Programs, 1978	2	100.0
Total	94	103.1*

*None of the decision packages contains additional salary requests for existing positions as these are established by the governor for all state employees and then inserted in the final budget request. As a consequence, in all cases, the cumulative percentages of the decision packages submitted are somewhat lower than they would actually be if salary-policy money were included.

Source: Departmental Data.

In choosing among the various options presented to them, the committee generally accepted those options that resulted in a clearer, simpler, and more flexible bill than HB 501 had been. Specifically, for example, the committee accepted the program level rather than the activity level as the decision unit. The implication that separate decision packages had to be developed at various organizational levels was deleted. Additionally, the minimum level of funding mandated in the proposal was less than 91 percent. The proposal went on to empower the Joint Committee on Appropriations to select up to a maximum of six departments, divisions, or offices to use the ZBB format.

Subsequently, this proposal was introduced in the fifty-third session of the legislature, which began on January 3, 1978. The bill (SB 47) was referred to the Joint Committee on Appropriations, where on January 25, 1978, the committee refused to send the bill out to the floor, by a 12-7 vote. Reportedly, this action upset the Republican legislative leadership. In any event, on January 26, 1978, the bill was reconsidered and, by a 14-to-4 vote, sent out with a "Do pass" recommendation. The bill easily passed both houses and was signed into law by the governor on February 13, 1978. As provided for in the new law, the Joint Appropriations Committee selected the Division of Elementary and Secondary Education of the Department of Education and Cultural Affairs to prepare its FY 1980 request using the ZBB format.

On a second front, having prepared a pilot zero-base budget, the department still had to go through the regular program-budget preparation and review process. Fortunately, much of the information used in preparing the zero-base budget request could be used as well in preparing a program-budget request, without a great deal of additional work (the one notable exception was the Law Enforcement Program of the Highway Patrol, where the seven activities included in ZBB now had to be consolidated again into a single program).

On September 22, 1978, from 1:00 to 3:00 p.m., the Department of Public Safety had its formal budget hearing before the Bureau of Finance and Management. Representatives of the Joint Appropriations Committee and their staff were also in attendance. At this hearing, there was some discussion focused much more on policy questions that transcended individual decision packages. Based upon this hearing, the material provided to the Budget Office, and informal contacts with the Budget Office and the Governor's Office, the governor recommended a total FY 1979 budget of $14,281,212 for Public Safety, and 436.5 FTE employees. This recommendation was presented in the governor's Budget Book in program-budget terms, although the decision package that most closely approximated the governor's recommendation for a particular program was identified. As backup material for the recommended program-budget request, the Bureau of Finance and Management also prepared a recommended line-item breakdown for each program.

Thus, when the department appeared before Subcommittee 1 of the Joint Appropriations Committee on December 14, 1977, the commitee had, in effect, three different budget formats to examine: ZBB, the program budget, and the object line-item budget. As a consequence, a considerable amount of time during the hearing was devoted to identifying where in each budget format the request for a particular program could be found. The department also made a very brief appearance before Subcommittee 1 on January 10, 1978. In neither appearance, nor in what was reported of the Appropriations Committee's deliberations, did the zero-base information play a significant role in committee decisions regarding the department's budget. Ultimately, the committee recommended, and the legislature approved, a FY 1979 funding level of $14,845,028 for the department, and 436.9 FTE employees.

CONCLUSIONS AND RECOMMENDATIONS

In concluding this study, one point should be made immediately: contrary to early concerns, partisan politics were not a factor in the ZBB pilot project. Rather, all participants in the process made a genuine effort to study ZBB from the vantage point of whether or not this budget approach could improve budget decisions in South Dakota.

More generally, in reflecting upon South Dakota's experience with ZBB, three recommendations to any jurisdiction preparing to adopt ZBB, particularly through legislation or an ordinance, can be offered. The first recommendation is to keep any approach simple and flexible, by defining only the key concepts of ZBB, such as decision units, decision packages, and the ranking process. In keeping the approach simple and flexible, these concepts should be formulated in a manner that is as consistent as possible with the current budgeting system used in the jurisdiction. By taking this approach, the proliferation of new forms can be avoided, as can the tendency to concentrate on the forms and procedures of ZBB rather than on the substance of the budget request. Utilizing the current system as much as possible also will increase the chances of having the necessary data to support the ZBB process.

In a like manner, mandating an arbitrary percentage of the current year's budget as the minimum level, which the first decision package cannot exceed, should be avoided at least until managers have shown that they will not prepare decision packages at below current-year funding. If an arbitrary percentage must be established, it should be less than 90 percent of current-year funding. The problem with any set percentage at all, but particularly a percentage sharply below current-year funding, is that set percentage will not set a realistic minimum for all activities or programs of an agency. Particularly, if the required minimum is sharply below current-year funding, the result will tend to be a minimum level that is not realistic, followed by a second level, which is the current level. The real minimum level will end up not being identified, and decision makers will not have the necessary information to make an intelligent decision as to whether or not to reduce the current-year funding for a particular program.

In addition, arbitrary minimums that are sharply below current levels can create morale problems as large numbers of personnel are slated for elimination at the minimum level of funding. Any adverse impact on morale would be justified if this minimum level were a realistic one, but where the minimum level is unrealistic, there is no gain in good management information to offset the loss of morale that occurs when reductions in force are discussed.

Second, in addition to keeping the approach simple and flexible, in the initial stages, ZBB should be applied only to a few agencies. The mechanics of ZBB are sufficiently different from those of other budgeting systems, and the process sufficiently complex, so that it will require a trial period for a jurisdiction's officials to decide, first, whether ZBB is in fact the system they wish to use, and, if so, in precisely what format they wish to use it. From this perspective, to put all agencies on ZBB immediately will, at best, waste a lot of time and, at worst, might endanger the whole approach as agencies feel frustrated and overwhelmed by this new approach. In selecting pilot agencies, the principal aim should be to secure a group of agencies diverse enough to ensure, as best one can, that the experience of these agencies during the test phase will be transferable to all agencies in the jurisdiction.

The third recommendation regarding the setting up of ZBB is to allow enough time for it and to provide enough training. Selecting only a limited number of agencies will tend to accomplish this result for most agencies in the implementing jurisdiction, but, if the test period of ZBB is to be of maximum value, it is also essential for the pilot agencies to have sufficient time and training. The time allotted to the project in South Dakota was not sufficient. Thus, as an example, the Department of Public Safety was forced to prepare decision packages for FY 1979 without the benefit of final expenditure data for FY 1977. Obviously, the absence of final FY 1977 expenditures made projecting FY 1979 needs more difficult. Then, too, as previously mentioned, more time should have been spent understanding the rational used by the division directors in ranking decision packages within their division, and in explaining to them (and to the Budget Office and the Appropriations Committee) the rationale used by the secretary in preparing the final departmental ranking. While the minimum time required for the pilot agencies participating in ZBB would vary, depending upon such factors as staff resources, five months would appear to be the absolute minimum time that should be allowed for training and implementing ZBB the first time around.

As to whether or not a jurisdiction should adopt ZBB, the only answer can be that it depends upon a number of factors. First, it depends upon the jurisdiction's current budgetary system. If the current system provides decision makers with the necessary information to help make the value judgments that are the essence of the budget decision-making process, then there is no need to consider adopting ZBB simply because ZBB is in in budgeting circles. On the other hand, if the current budget system is a poor one, then, by all means, the adoption of ZBB should be seriously considered. Similarly, if the current budget system has become stale and mechanical with usage, adoption of ZBB ought to be carefully examined, because the adoption of any new system (including ZBB) forces one to rethink, and either change or reaffirm, many basic budgetary and managerial decisions.

Second, whether or not to adopt ZBB depends upon what one is trying to accomplish with a budgetary system. Thus, if budget reductions are the goal, ZBB is no sure way to achieve this goal. In explaining ZBB as used in Texas, to the first meeting of the South Dakota Zero-Base Budgeting Study Committee, Oliver, of the Texas Legislative Council, put it best when he pointed out that ZBB by itself will not save or spend money, because a conservative can use ZBB to restrain costs while a liberal can use it to expand budgets. To put the same point in a slightly different form, one's political philosophy of government is far more important than one's budgetary technique in determining the size of government.

Additionally, if one wishes to curtail the growth of government, probably it is more important to change the reward structure in which government officials operate. So long as administrators are compensated financially and in status terms, on the principle that bigger is better, no budget system, for very long at least, will produce significant savings.

At the same time, if one's goal is to involve more people farther down in the organization in the budget-preparation process, ZBB will help accomplish this goal. Obviously, other budget systems could involve program people as well, but ZBB, more than most systems, compels program-manager involvement. In the South Dakota experience, this aspect of ZBB was invariably recognized as one of the pluses in the experiment.

Furthermore, if one's goal in the budget process is to place the emphasis on questions of efficiency rather than on those of effectiveness, then ZBB is an approach worth considering. Conversely, if one is more concerned with attempting to assess program effectiveness, ZBB may not be as helpful as other budgeting systems, such as program budgeting. In theory, of course, there is nothing in ZBB that precludes giving consideration to questions of effectiveness as well as to those of efficiency. However, as a practical matter, given limited time, and given ZBB's emphasis on smaller units of analysis, the emphasis on efficiency will no doubt occur in reality. Indeed, the very idea of talking about different levels of funding of subprogram elements puts one at a level of analysis where considerations of efficiency are easier to deal with than considerations of effectiveness.

Finally, in considering whether or not to adopt ZBB, it should be noted that ZBB is a complex system to administer. The ranking of decision packages is an example of the complexity. Obviously, ranking decision packages involves value judgments. Hence, for the process to work at its best, at each level, care must be taken to discover and understand the perspective from which a given person is ranking decision packages. If this is not done, and lower-level rankings are either automatically accepted or summarily rejected, then those who should be establishing broad direction for the agency are either abdicating their responsibility, on the one hand, or exercising their responsibility in an arbitrary and a capricious manner, on the other hand.

Another example of the complexity of the process is the interrelationship of decision packages for different programs. For instance, to keep to a minimum funding level in one decision package, the department proposed to cut out its mailroom. In actuality, of course, Public Safety would continue to need some way to send and receive mail. In this illustration, the burden for continuing this service would have fallen on the Bureau of Administration. To be sure—in this example, as well as in the countless other examples that would occur—that impacts of maintaining the funding level of a program are reflected in funding levels of other programs would be a most important but most difficult task. Thus, the sophistication of the central budget office in the process is another important consideration in deciding whether or not to adopt ZBB.

In examining the budget system in South Dakota in light of these considerations, one has a ready explanation as to why ZBB has received a lukewarm reception to date. In comparison with the program-budgeting system currently used in the state, the ZBB approach did not improve budget decision making within the Department of Public Safety, in the Budget Office, or within the Appropriations Committee. The fact of the matter is that departmental managers were aware of

the major problems and opportunities facing the department prior to
ZBB.

A further fact is that gaps or duplications in the delivery of resources that might be discovered through the ZBB approach were already being discovered through the current budget-review process,
as well as through the annual policy-formulation process used by the
governor and through the three cabinet subgroups (Human Resources,
Economic Development, and Natural Resources) that meet on a regular
basis throughout the year. Perhaps in a larger jurisdiction, mechanisms such as these would not be sufficient to ensure coordination
and minimize duplication and service-delivery gaps. However, in
South Dakota, at the present time, these mechanisms seem to be
working, thereby lessening the need for ZBB.

Looking at the current budget system with a view toward keeping
the cost of government services as low as possible, the present system, again, seems to be working in a satisfactory manner. For example, the legislature, in producing the FY 1977 budget for the state
government, entirely eliminated three programs (Alcohol Safety Action, Weather Modification, and the Crop and Livestock Reporting
Service). For FY 1978, the administration proposed eliminating or
sharply curtailing the State Banking Examination Program and the
Insurance Program. Prior to the advent of ZBB, within the Department of Public Safety, the number of FTE personnel in the Driver
License Issuance Program had been cut from 18.5 to 12.0 while the
personnel in the Proration and Reciprocity Program were cut from
13.6 to 7.0.

In short, given the fact that ZBB cannot guarantee budget cuts,
and given the further fact that the current system is producing selective cuts, the budget-reduction appeal of ZBB is not especially
great in South Dakota.

Comparing the current budget system to ZBB in terms of se-
curing greater involvement of program managers in the budget process, there is no doubt that more program personnel were involved
in using ZBB, and there is no doubt that most division directors felt
this greater involvement to be worthwhile. However, given this perception, there is no reason why program personnel cannot continue
to have greater participation in the budget process under the program-
budgeting system.

As previously noted, ZBB tends to focus budgetary decision
making on questions of efficiency, rather than on those of effectiveness, to a greater degree than does program budgeting. It is also fair
to say that there is a growing tendency in South Dakota to emphasize
efficiency in program operations. In this situation, the appeal of ZBB
compared to program budgeting should be quite powerful and indeed
it might be, were it not for the fact that South Dakota has begun using

another budget tool to deal with efficiency questions, that is, the object line-item approach. This approach is one that is familiar to the actors involved and appears at this point to be preferable to ZBB in getting at the problem of efficiency. Given this relative satisfaction with the current budget system, the additional factor of the complexity of ZBB is also not attractive to decision makers. This is especially true of the Appropriations Committee, operating as it does in the context of alternating 30-day and 45-day sessions.

As other jurisdictions look at ZBB in light of their situations, they might well reach a different conclusion, because, to repeat, the decision to adopt ZBB should depend on the circumstances in a particular jurisdiction rather than on some absolute truth that ZBB is inherently good or bad.

Given this need to analyze ZBB in light of the current situation in a given jurisdiction, the final recommendation would be that a moratorium be placed on using the term zero-base budgeting. No one suggests in fact, starting from zero in the preparation of decision packages; so, in fact, the term is incorrect. That fact alone should excise the phrase from our vocabulary. Unfortunately, the use of ZBB is not simply incorrect, but it is insidious in its effect on a rational analysis of whether the approach embodied in ZBB will work in a particular jurisdiction. After all, who could be against a zero-base approach to governmental budgeting? Only some free-spending liberal who wants to foster waste and raise taxes. Fearing this will be the reaction, the public debate on ZBB is muted or nonexistent. Instead, the analysis and discussion on the adoption of ZBB, or any budget system, should be open and vigorous.

It is hoped that the comments in this chapter will assist jurisdictions in an open and vigorous discussion in regard to selecting the best budget system, given their situation and needs.

NOTES

1. See Aaron Wildavsky, The Politics of the Budgetary Process, 2d. ed. (Boston: Little, Brown, 1974), pp. 181-82; he notes: "Program budgeting has no standard definition. The general idea is that budgetary decisions should be made by focusing on output categories like governmental goals, objectives and end products instead of inputs like personnel, equipment and maintenance." In the South Dakota context, program budgeting can be defined as a system in which budget recommendations and decisions are made at the program level based upon an analysis both of input factors, such as personnel and capital assets, and output measures, as identified in performance indicators that are expressed in both efficiency and effectiveness terms.

The roots of program budgeting in South Dakota go back at least as far as 1966, when, under the administration of Republican Governor Nils Boe and his budget officer, Loren Carlson, the use of programs as the budgetary decision unit began. However, it was the Kneip administration that matured this system into full bloom as the decision-making system for budget allocations in the state.

2. Peter A. Phyrr, "The Zero-Base Approach to Government Budgeting," Public Administration Review, January-February 1977, pp. 1-8.

3. Peter A. Phyrr, Zero-Base Budgeting: A Practical Management Tool For Evaluation Expenses (New York: John Wiley and Sons, 1973).

4. While not entirely clear, it may have been that the authors of the law were attempting to provide for the consolidation of decision packages to reduce the workload for upper levels of management, because the scheme in the bill in some respects appears to be following a consolidation process outlined in Phyrr, Zero-Base Budgeting: A Practical Management Tool for Evaluation Expenses, op. cit. , chap. 5. At the same time, Phyrr's consolidation process does not call for developing new decision packages at each level. Phyrr also notes, "These cutoff guidelines were misunderstood in several of the agencies in Georgia, and some managers were forced to identify minimum level of effort packages at 60% for each activity" (p. 85). In the same way, the authors of HB 501 also may have misunderstood the consolidation process.

5. Phyrr, "A Zero-Base Approach to Government Budgeting," op. cit.

6. Minutes of the June 10, 1977 meeting of the Zero Base-Budgeting Study Committee (Pierre, S. D. : Legislative Research Council, 1977).

7

IMPLEMENTING
ZERO-BASE BUDGETING:
THE NEW ORLEANS
EXPERIENCE

Edward J. Clynch

Public budgeting in the United States has been subjected to numerous reform efforts throughout this century. A major purpose of many of these innovations is to improve the quality of budgeting choices in the face of competing demands for scarce resources. Attempts have been made to add or delete participants involved in the process, to alter participants' roles and/or to change the impact of roles on budgetary decisions, to improve the information serving as the basis of budgetary choices, and to incorporate analytic techniques into budgetary decision making.[1]

Zero-base budgeting (ZBB) is the reform instrument presently being utilized by many state and local jurisdictions and the federal government. The pace at which this tool is being adopted has created a need to ascertain the factors potentially affecting its successful implementation and its impact on budgetary decision making. Most writings about ZBB, however, are proscriptive, suggesting procedures to be followed, delineating possible problems officials may need to overcome, and pointing out potential benefits governments can attain through implementation.[2] There have been only a few investigations into the experiences of governments grappling with this budget reform.[3]

Edward J. Clynch is assistant professor of political science at Kansas State University. This chapter is a revision of a paper Clynch delivered at the annual meeting of the Midwest Political Science Association, April 20–22, 1977, Chicago. The author wishes to express his thanks to Michael McDonald for his very helpful comments on an earlier draft.

These initial examinations of zero-base budgeting in practice are a good start, but more research is necessary. In particular, there is a need to determine the perspectives of program and budget personnel at both the central administrative and departmental levels. The support of each role involved in budgeting is necessary for reform to succeed. Thus it is unlikely that a permanent change in a jurisdiction's budgeting format will materialize if cooperation is absent from any group of participants. [4]

Allen Schick indicates, moreover, that variations in roles being filled by budget players may influence their feelings about alterations in the budget process. In essence, persons holding different positions might be expected to react in diverse ways to zero-base budgeting since its impact on their functions could vary. [5] To date, no attempt had been made to discern the similarities and/or differences in the impressions about zero-base budgeting held by actors carrying out various roles. This study is a beginning effort at filling this void, by reporting on the perspectives of persons involved in the implementation of ZBB in New Orleans. It addresses a number of pertinent questions. Do persons performing different functions perceive the same roadblocks to successful ZBB implementation? What are the feelings of these practitioners about the commitment of top management to this process? Do they have similar perceptions about whether or not zero-base budgeting increases central administrative control over both nonbudgetary and budgetary decisions? Do they have similar views about benefits resulting from the process? Finally, is there variation among participants in terms of personal commitment to zero-base budgeting?

Information and data for this study have been gathered through a review of pertinent documents, personal observation of working sessions, in-depth interviews with relevant actors from each participating department and the Chief Administrative Office (CAO) of the New Orleans government, and a questionnaire administered to all persons involved with zero-base budgeting at both the departmental and CAO levels.

The first section is a brief overview of ZBB procedures utilized by New Orleans. The second section compares and contrasts similarities and differences in viewpoints of participants performing different roles.

THE NEW ORLEANS ZERO-BASE FORMAT

The impetus behind zero-base budgeting in New Orleans differed from that of most jurisdictions adopting this format. The catalyst was not the mayor or other persons in executive authority, but, rather, the City Council. The council desired more information to aid in the priority ranking of budgeting decisions in a time of financial constraint. This desire was particularly strong among the new councilmen who took office just as the budget for FY 1977 was being approved in November 1976.*

An ordinance was approved on December 1, 1976, specifying the general outline of the ZBB process.[6] During 1977, a ZBB pilot program was instituted in the Civil Service, Fire, Health, and Streets Departments; and in 1978 the city expanded the initial steps of this process to include all departments.

There is no right way to carry out zero-base budgeting. Advocates indicate a format should be designed to suit the requirements of the implementing government.[7] Nevertheless, there seems to be agreement on what constitutes the basic elements of the process. Key steps are the designation of budgetary decision units, the formulation of decision packages for each decision unit, and the ranking of decision packages in order of their priority, first by the decision unit and then by the central administration.[8]

Original City Council expectations generally conformed with this format, but the actual implementation guidelines developed by the CAO in July 1977 called for a more limited undertaking during the initial year.[9] In the light of several constraints, general agreement was reached between the council and the city administration to modify council requirements. Departments were operating under severe time limitations. Both a zero-base budget and a regular line-item budget had to be prepared in three months. There also was a lack of quantifiable information at the departmental level. Finally, there was the desire to keep the paperwork to a minimum and thus make completion an attainable goal.

The designation of ZBB decision units in New Orleans did follow the format used by many other jurisdictions. The divisions within each department that serves as a budget unit for the regular budget process were utilized as zero-base decision units. Thus, like many other governments, New Orleans confined the basic ZBB operating units to its existing organizational structure.

The formulation of decision packages in New Orleans did differ from what has been done by most other governments, however. De-

---

*Due to a federal court suit concerning racial gerrymandering, the election of City Council members was postponed for three years. When the suit was resolved, a special election was held immediately, resulting in three new councilmen taking office during the time the council was considering the budget.

cision packages are mechanisms for justifying different levels of funding for decision units. Figure 7.1 shows the two ways the decision package normally is formulated. One possibility links, in quantifiable terms, the level of services provided with a given amount of

FIGURE 7.1

Decision-Package Formats

Source: Compiled by the author.

resources. The second format indicates the extent to which goals or objectives can be achieved with a particular level of service performance. Each decision package would include a quantifiable objective, the level of service performance needed to achieve the stated objective, and the resources required to carry out the specified level of service.

The procedure adopted by New Orleans, displayed in Table 7.1, does not link resources to service performance or objectives achieved. Thus, unlike what is normally thought of as zero-base budgeting, New Orleans did not require the costing out of individual services and/or objectives, a requisite if choices from among objectives are to be made directly through the budget process. Budget units needed only to supply overall man-year requirements and object-classification dollar figures for each service level. Table 7.2 displays the format utilized by budget units to report man-years and dollar amounts.

Each budget unit was expected, however, to link different levels of service performance with varying degrees of accomplished results. It was necessary to specify the quantifiable outcomes achievable when services were performed at 70 percent, 90 percent, and 100 percent of current levels. Each unit also was asked to indicate measurable results obtainable when service performance was at an expansion level determined by the department. Table 7.3 displays the format utilized to tie service performance to the attainment of objectives at each service level.

Indeed, the levels in Tables 7.2 and 7.3 are service levels, and not expenditure levels. Thus, references to 100 percent would indicate

TABLE 7.1

Zero-Base Budgeting Procedure Adopted by New Orleans, 1977

Resources	Activities*	Objectives
Listed only for budget unit	Activity Activity Activity	Objective (1)
	Activity Activity Activity	Objective (2)
	Activity Activity Activity	Objective (3)

*Activities are not ranked.
Source: Compiled by the author.

the dollars needed to maintain the present level of services, even though, due to inflation, an increase in spending would be required. References to other service levels also reflect percentages of activity performance, and not a percentage of dollars spent.

The final step in zero-base budgeting is the ranking of decision packages. Decision units rank their packages in order of importance, according to their priorities. The central administration then reviews departmental rankings submitted by all decision units and formulates a governmentwide ranking. An effort is made to finance as many decision packages, from this list, as can be accommodated with the revenues projected for the upcoming year.

During the initial year of the ZBB process New Orleans did not combine service levels of various objectives into a single rank order. Instead, budget units and departments were only asked to rank-order objectives in the order of their importance. The CAO, moreover, did not alter the rankings of objectives submitted by the participating departments. Since line personnel believe that the majority of objectives are currently being achieved to some extent, it is logical to assume budget units would not, if forced, choose one objective over another. Instead, the choice probably would be to achieve partially each objective.

TABLE 7.2

Required Dollar Amounts and Man-Years by Service Level, by Budget Unit

Department: FIRE
Org. Title: FIRE TRAINING

Classification of Expenditure	1978 Requested Budget			
	70 Percent Level	90 Percent Level	Current Level	Expansion Level
Personal Services	$160,292	$160,292	$172,178	$241,684
Contractual Services	1,900	2,000	2,100	21,850
Supplies and Materials	4,750	4,800	5,000	14,435
Equipment and Property	0	0	500	21,535
Other charges	0	0	0	0
Total expenditures	$166,942	$167,092	$179,778	$299,504
Man years				
CETA	0	0	0	0
General Fund	10	10	10	15
Total	10	10	10	15

Source: Compiled by the author.

TABLE 7.3

Objectives and Activities by Service Level

Department: FIRE
Org. Title: FIRE TRAINING

Objectives and Activity Statements	Service Level			
	70 Percent	90 Percent	Current	Expansion
To conduct ____ training classes for industry and institutions on fire prevention and extinguishers or other fire-related subjects. To aid in the prevention of fire.	14	18	20	25
To conduct fire-prevention and extinguisher presentation to industry and institutions for ____ hours	56	72	80	80
To conduct presentations on rescue drags and carriers, and air-mask classes to industry and institutions for ____ hours	0	0	0	20

Source: Compiled by the author.

With zero-base procedures, New Orleans also established a review team for each department and an implementation team at the CAO level. The review teams were composed of the CAO budget analyst normally assigned to the department, the chief departmental budget analyst, and one CAO staff member from the program-development section and one CAO staff member from the program-evaluation section. Review teams were to review departmental submittals and make recommendations for changes to the department before the final product was sent to the CAO. The implementation team was composed of the chief budget analyst from the CAO budget section, two persons from the program-development section, and one from the program-evaluation section. The implementation team was expected to coordinate the efforts of departmental review teams, settle any procedural and programmatic disputes, and review the ZBB budgets submitted by the departments from the CAO perspective. [10]

The formal utilized by New Orleans gave program developers and evaluators direct input into the formulation of the ZBB budget. Thus, actors not previously involved in the budget process were formally admitted to budgetary decision making. If New Orleans continues zero-base budgeting with these persons as participants, it is likely that departments will be forced to develop more precise quantifiable measures for utilization in the budget process. The tasks performed by these individuals place heavy stress on quantification. Moreover, many programmers (interviewed by the author) believe that the creation of measures relating activities performed to objectives achieved within this budget process can enhance the evaluation of ongoing programs. The following section explores the differences in viewpoints about ZBB expressed by participants fulfilling different roles, including those persons brought into the process because of this new format.

PARTICIPANTS' PERCEPTIONS OF ZERO-BASE BUDGETING

A major shortcoming of previous investigations into the implementation of zero-base budgeting has been the lack of a systematic and comprehensive evaluation of participants' perceptions about this format. This section is an effort to remedy this void by comparing and contrasting viewpoints of program and budget personnel from participating departments and the CAO in New Orleans. It focuses on perspectives about difficulties faced during implementation, the commitment of top management to ZBB, changes and potential changes in the relationships between departments and the central administration due to this format, the benefits and potential benefits accruing from this undertaking, and the personal commitment of individual participants to zero-base budgeting.[11]

For the purposes of this analysis, participants who were interviewed are divided by position. They include departmental line supervisors (including department heads), departmental budget analysts, CAO programmers, and CAO budget analysts. In some areas there may not be major differences in viewpoints among the persons fulfilling these roles. For instance, participants, regardless of position, may perceive the same difficulties standing in the way of successful implementation. Previous ZBB implementation studies do not systematically review the perspectives of all the participants included in this study. These initial findings, however, do not reveal any major differences in difficulties encountered by practitioners holding different positions.[12] In other areas there is no logical basis to assume that perspectives are either diverse or uniform. It is unclear, for example, whether differences would emerge in feelings about the commitment to ZBB of top management and the effect of ZBB on departmental-CAO relationships. Variations of viewpoints could be expected to emerge concerning some points, however; CAO program-development and program-evaluation personnel might be more likely than other participants to have positive feelings about zero-base budgeting, given their familiarity with making decisions on the basis of quantifiable measures, and their desire for program evaluation. Thus it would not be surprising if these persons have a greater tendency to believe ZBB is producing or will produce meaningful benefits for the city. Furthermore, they are probably more committed to this process than other participants who generally are not oriented to such a decision-making process.

Chi-square is used in this study to determine whether or not there are statistically significant differences revealed among the different positions. The measures of association used are phi in the two-by-two case and Cramer's V for all other tables. Phi has a straightforward interpretation, with phi-squared being the percentage of the variance explained. Cramer's V is selected because it is the appropriate statistic when tables contain both nominal and ordinal data. Its magnitude in and of itself is difficult to interpret; however, the magnitude of Cramer's V for one table can reasonably be compared to phi or Cramer's V in all other tables.[13]

Difficulties Facing Zero-Base Budgeting Participants

Participants were queried about the difficulties they encountered in implementing ZBB; the results are reported in Tables 7.4-7.12. As can be seen, New Orleans generally faced the same problems found

TABLE 7.4

What Was the Effect of ZBB on Time and Effort Participant
Spent on Budget Preparation?

	Participants			
Response	Line Personnel	Departmental Budget Analysts	CAO Budget Analysts	CAO Programmers
Increased time	92.3%	100.0%	100.0%	91.7%
The same or less time	7.7	0.0	0.0	8.3
Total	100.0 (26)	100.0 (8)	100.0 (5)	100.0 (12)

Note: X^2 = 1.09655 (P = .779); Cramer's V = 0.146.
Source: Compiled by the author.

TABLE 7.5

Was There Adequate Advanced Planning by the Chief
Administrative Office?

	Participants			
Response	Line Personnel	Departmental Budget Analysts	CAO Budget Analysts	CAO Programmers
Yes	11.5%	12.5%	0.0%	14.3%
Uncertain	19.2	0.0	0.0	14.3
No	69.2	87.5	100.0	71.4
Total	100.0 (26)	100.0 (8)	100.0 (5)	100.0 (14)

Note: X^2 = 3.84560 (P = .698); Cramer's V = .190.
Source: Compiled by the author.

113

TABLE 7. 6

Were Adequate Instructions Issued by the
Chief Administrative Office?

| Response | Participants | | | |
	Line Personnel	Departmental Budget Analysts	CAO Budget Analysts	CAO Programmers
Yes	15.4%	25.0%	0.0%	18.2%
Uncertain	7.7	0.0	50.0	36.2
No	76.9	75.0	50.0	45.5
Total	100.0 (26)	100.0 (8)	100.0 (4)	100.0 (11)

Note: X^2 = .1042055 (P = .108); Cramer's V = .326.
Source: Compiled by the author.

TABLE 7. 7

Was There Adequate Information on Man-Years Needed
to Carry out Activities?

| Response | Participants | | | |
	Line Personnel	Departmental Budget Analysts	CAO Budget Analysts	CAO Programmers
Yes	42.3%	12.5%	40.0%	0.0%
Uncertain	30.8	37.5	0.0	23.1
No	26.9	50.0	60.0	76.9
Total	100.0 (26)	100.0 (8)	100.0 (5)	100.0 (13)

Note: X^2 = 13.59762 (P = .035)*
Cramer's V = .362
*Significant at the .05 level
Source: Compiled by the author.

TABLE 7.8

Was There Adequate Information on Costs of Resources
Needed to Carry out Activities?

	Participants			
Response	Line Personnel	Departmental Budget Analysts	CAO Budget Analysts	CAO Programmers
Yes	46. 2%	25. 0%	40. 0%	0. 0%
Uncertain	26. 9	0. 0	20. 0	15. 4
No	26. 9	75. 0	40. 0	84. 6
Total	100. 0 (26)	100. 0 (8)	100. 0 (5)	100. 0 (13)

Note: X^2 = 15. 64962 (P = . 016)*
    Cramer's V = . 388
    *Significant at the . 05 level
Source: Compiled by the author.

TABLE 7.9

Was There Adequate Information on the Extent to Which
Services Accomplish Measurable Results?

	Participants			
Response	Line Personnel	Departmental Budget Analysts	CAO Budget Analysts	CAO Programmers
Yes	53. 8%	37. 5%	20. 0%	0. 0%
Uncertain	15. 4	25. 0	40. 0	23. 1
No	30. 3	37. 5	40. 0	76. 9
Total	100. 0 (26)	100. 0 (8)	100. 0 (5)	100. 0 (13)

Note: X^2 = 13. 24152 (P = . 039)*
    Cramer's V = . 357
    *Significant at the . 05 level
Source: Compiled by the author.

TABLE 7.10

Did Chief Administrative Office Personnel
Understand ZBB Procedures?

	Participants			
Response	Line Personnel	Departmental Budget Analysts	CAO Budget Analysts	CAO Programmers
Yes	7.7%	25.0%	40.0%	35.7%
Uncertain	38.5	12.5	0.0	28.6
No	53.8	62.5	60.0	35.7
Total	100.0 (26)	100.0 (8)	100.0 (5)	100.0 (14)

Note: X^2 = 8.64890 (P = .194); Cramer's V = .286.
Source: Compiled by the author.

TABLE 7.11

Did Department Heads Understand
ZBB Procedures?

	Participants			
Response	Line Personnel (Department Heads Excluded)	Departmental Budget Analysts	CAO Budget Analysts	CAO Programmers
Yes	12.5%	50.0%	0.0%	14.3%
Uncertain	16.7	25.0	40.0	35.7
No	70.8	25.0	60.0	50.0
Total	100.0 (24)	100.0 (8)	100.0 (5)	100.0 (14)

Note: X^2 = 10.17498 (P = .118); Cramer's V = .316.
Source: Compiled by the author.

TABLE 7.12

Did Participants Personally Understand ZBB Procedures?

	Participants			
Response	Line Personnel	Departmental Budget Analysts	CAO Budget Analysts	CAO Programmers
Yes	36.0%	25.0%	40.0%	57.1%
Uncertain	16.0	12.5	20.0	14.3
No	52.2	62.5	40.0	28.6
Total	100.0 (25)	100.0 (8)	100.0 (5)	100.0 (14)

Note: $X^2 = 3.17165$ (P = .787); Cramer's V = .175.
Source: Compiled by the author.

to exist elsewhere. Persons fulfilling different roles, moreover, have similar views of the problems encountered, with the exception of the adequacy of information provided to ZBB participants.

Table 7.4 shows a general consensus that ZBB increased time and effort spent on budget preparation. Tables 7.5 and 7.6 indicate that most participants in each position felt advanced planning by the CAO and the instructions issued by this unit were not sufficient for the task at hand. Participants, furthermore, tended to believe the CAO and department heads did not understand the procedures being implemented, as shown in Tables 7.10 and 7.11. More CAO program personnel believed they personally understood the process than did participants fulfilling other roles, but the relationship is not significant (Table 7.12).

Lack of information has been found to be a difficulty facing participants in other jurisdictions adopting zero-base budgeting. Participants in New Orleans were asked their opinions about the adequacy of information on the costs of resources, the man years required to complete services, and the extent to which activities being performed are accomplishing measurable results. As can be seen in Tables 7.7-7.9, information inadequacies appear to be a problem, but significant differences in viewpoints exist among participants fulfilling different roles. In all cases, Cramer's V is .35 or better. Persons in departmental line positions are more likely than others to believe sufficient information is available. Conversely, individuals acting as CAO program developers and evaluators are the most pessimistic, with over 75 percent perceiving the state of current information as unsatisfactory in all instances. Thus persons actually carrying out programs are least concerned about informational problems, while those who plan and evaluate programs are most likely to view this as a hurdle to successful ZBB implementation. One suspects the perceptions of the planners and evaluators are closer to reality since their functions give them greater familiarity with the problems of quantifiable measures.

Commitment to Zero-Base Budgeting

Another factor often associated with the long-range success of a budget innovation is the commitment to it of those involved in the budget process. Bureaucratic resistance to change is likely to surface if persons in authority are perceived as not caring about successful implementation.[14] Tables 7.13-7.16 indicate the feelings participants have concerning the commitment to ZBB of top management.

The results are mixed. There is general agreement, however, that the City Council is committed to ZBB—which is hardly surprising, since ZBB was started through a council initiative (Table 7.13). The commitment of former Mayor Landrieu is open to question, however. A large segment of persons filling each role are uncertain of the stand he took (Table 7.14). Generally, participants believe the CAO and department heads are committed to ZBB, although line supervisors are less certain about this than others (Tables 7.15 and 7.16). It is hard to draw any conclusions about the impact of commitment on long-range success since perceptions concern only the first year. The responses confirm, however, a general perception that top management, with the exception of Landrieu, supported this budget change. Since Landrieu has been replaced by Ernest Morial, however, Landrieu's stand is not likely to affect participants in the future. The new mayor has indicated his support for zero-base budgeting by continuing the process. Clearly, there is no feeling that top management views zero-based budgeting as merely an exercise.

Effect of Zero-Base Budgeting on the Ongoing Relationships between Departments and the Central Administration

Advocates of budgetary reform assume changing procedures will have a bearing on the conduct of budgetary affairs.[15] One major change in New Orleans is the addition of CAO program planners and

TABLE 7.13

Was City Council Committed to ZBB?

Response	Participants			
	Line Personnel	Departmental Budget Analysts	CAO Budget Analysts	CAO Programmers
Committed	64.0%	87.5%	80.0%	85.7%
Uncertain	32.0	12.5	20.0	14.3
Uncommitted	4.0	0.0	0.0	0.0
Total	100.0 (25)	100.0 (8)	100.0 (5)	100.0 (14)

Note: X^2 = .362071 (P = .728); Cramer's V = .187.
Source: Compiled by the author.

TABLE 7.14

Was Mayor Landrieu Committed to ZBB?

Response	Participants			
	Line Personnel	Departmental Budget Analysts	CAO Budget Analysts	CAO Programmers
Committed	32.0%	50.0%	40.0%	28.6%
Uncertain	56.0	37.5	40.0	64.3
Uncommitted	12.0	12.5	20.0	7.1
Total	100.0 (25)	100.0 (8)	100.0 (5)	100.0 (14)

Note: X^2 = 2.22164 (P = .898); Cramer's V = .46.
Source: Compiled by the author.

119

TABLE 7. 15

Was Chief Administrative Office Committed to ZBB?

		Participants		
Response	Line Personnel	Departmental Budget Analysts	CAO Budget Analysts	CAO Programmers
Committed	36. 0%	62. 5%	80. 0%	78. 6%
Uncertain	60. 0	37. 5	20. 0	21. 4
Uncommitted	4. 0	0. 0	0. 0	0. 0
Total	100. 0 (25)	100. 0 (8)	100. 0 (5)	100. 0 (14)

Note: $X^2 = 8.65260$ (P = .194); Cramer's V = .288.
Source: Compiled by the author.

TABLE 7. 16

Were Department Heads Committed to ZBB?

		Participants		
Response	Line Personnel (Department Heads Excluded)	Departmental Budget Analysts	CAO Budget Analysts	CAO Programmers
Committed	39. 1%	100. 0%	75. 0%	78. 6%
Uncertain	47. 8	0. 0	25. 0	14. 3
Uncommitted	13. 0	0. 0	0. 0	7. 1
Total	100. 0 (23)	100. 0 (8)	100. 0 (4)	100. 0 (14)

Note: $X^2 = 12.38605$ (P = 0.54); Cramer's V = .356.
Source: Compiled by the author.

evaluators to the budget process. Thus roles previously not directly involved in budgeting have been made part of the process. As noted above, their addition may in itself affect budget choices, especially in the long term.

Alternations in procedures could also affect the ongoing relationships between departments and the CAO, by expanding central administrative leverage over both nonbudgetary and budgetary decisions. CAO awareness of departmental programmatic preferences could be increased by requiring these units to specify objectives and to indicate how services being performed contribute to their achievement. In essence, awareness potentially could involve not only knowing the departmental objectives, but also the degree to which goals are being accomplished. Thus ZBB has the possibility of serving as an evaluation system and could assist the CAO with long-range planning and other nonbudgetary decisions.

The addition of this new information might also enable the CAO to make budgetary choices previously reached at the departmental level. One function of an objective-oriented budget system is to increase control over spending decisions by top management, thus making it reflect their priorities.

The effects of zero-base budgeting on the relationships between departments and the CAO can be seen in Tables 7.17-7.20. CAO personnel are more likely than persons within departments to believe the initial ZBB effort increased CAO awareness of departmental programmatic preferences, but the differences in viewpoints among the various participants is not significant. CAO personnel also have a greater tendency to perceive ZBB will improve CAO awareness in future years.

Turning to the impact of zero-base budgeting on CAO control (Table 7.19), it seems clear that growing CAO awareness is not automatically translated into increasing CAO control over budget decisions. Only a small minority of participants believe the initial effort increased CAO mastery of the budget. None of the CAO budget analysts perceived this to be the case. Overall, there is a tendency for participants occupying each position to feel that ZBB will increase CAO control in future years (Table 7.20). The most optimistic are the CAO programmers, 50.0 percent of whom believe ZBB will increase control. Among departmental personnel, however, a large number of people are uncertain about the ultimate impact of ZBB, with 41.7 percent of the line personnel and 42.9 percent of the departmental budget analysts unsure of the ultimate effect on CAO leverage over the budget.

One year is too short a time span to draw any definitive conclusions, but the increased awareness of departmental programmatic preferences has the potential to broaden central administrative influence over long-range planning and other nonbudgetary decisions. During the initial year this format did not seem to increase CAO

TABLE 7.17

Did ZBB Increase CAO Awareness of Departmental
Programmatic Preferences?

| Response | Line Personnel | Participants | | |
		Departmental Budget Analysts	CAO Budget Analysts	CAO Programmers
Yes	34.6%	50.0%	80.0%	71.4%
Uncertain	38.5	37.5	20.0	21.4
No	26.9	12.5	0.0	7.1
Total	100.0 (26)	100.0 (8)	100.0 (5)	100.0 (14)

Note: X^2 = 7.72503 (P = .259); Cramer's V = .270.
Source: Compiled by the author.

TABLE 7.18

Will ZBB, in the Future, Increase CAO Awareness of
Departmental Programmatic Preferences?

| Response | Line Personnel | Participants | | |
		Departmental Budget Analysts	CAO Budget Analysts	CAO Programmers
Yes	42.3%	62.5%	100.0%	78.6%
Uncertain	42.3	25.0	0.0	21.4
No	15.4	12.5	0.0	0.0
Total	100.0 (26)	100.0 (8)	100.0 (5)	100.0 (14)

Note: X^2 = 9.5935 (P = .146); Cramer's V = .300.
Source: Compiled by the author.

TABLE 7.19

Did ZBB Increase CAO Control over Budget Decisions?

		Participants		
Response	Line Personnel	Departmental Budget Analysts	CAO Budget Analysts	CAO Programmers
Yes	15.4%	14.3%	0.0%	21.4%
Uncertain	38.5	14.3	20.0	37.5
No	46.2	71.4	80.0	42.9
Total	100.0 (26)	100.0 (7)	100.0 (5)	100.0 (14)

Note: X^2 = 4.04309 (P = .671); Cramer's V = .197.
Source: Compiled by the author.

TABLE 7.20

Will ZBB Increase CAO Control in Future Years?

		Participants		
Response	Line Personnel	Departmental Budget Analysts	CAO Budget Analysts	CAO Programmers
Yes	29.2%	28.6%	40.0%	50.0%
Uncertain	41.7	42.9	20.0	42.9
No	29.2	28.6	40.0	7.1
Total	100.0 (24)	100.0 (7)	100.0 (5)	100.0 (14)

Note: X^2 = 4.28142 (P = .639); Cramer's V = .207.
Source: Compiled by the author.

control over budget choices, but the perception exists that CAO control may grow. Clearly, this procedure is believed to have the potential to decrease departmental mastery over budgetary decisions.

Benefits of Zero-Base Budgeting

Zero-base budgeting must have an impact on decision making if it is to be more than simply a group of techniques followed for the sake of form. Among the mentioned potential payoffs accruing to governments adopting this format are a more meaningful priority ranking of expenditures, the ability to provide more services without increasing costs, the ability to provide a better quality of services, and the generating of better management information than is possible with a line-item process. [16]

The use of ZBB to set priorities would normally mean using this procedure to change levels of support for various activities. Table 7.21 reports on the extent to which participants believe ZBB resulted in a shifting of resources among the functions performed by departments. There is general agreement that this technique did not lead to changes in spending. Thus at least during the initial year, zero-base budgeting has not benefited New Orleans in this manner.

TABLE 7.21

Did ZBB Result in a Shifting of Financial Resources among Department Functions?

		Participants		
Response	Line Personnel	Departmental Budget Analysts	CAO Budget Analysts	CAO Programmers
Great or some shifting	19.2%	0.0%	0.0%	15.4%
Uncertain	3.8	0.0	0.0	23.1
No apparent shifting	76.9	100.0	100.0	61.5
Total	100.0 (26)	100.0 (8)	100.0 (5)	100.0 (13)

Note: $X^2 = 9.17247$ (P = .164); Cramer's V = .297.
Source: Compiled by the author.

Another possible benefit of ZBB could be an expansion in services without a corresponding increase in spending. Most New Orleans participants do not believe this occurred during the initial year, however (Table 7.22). Nor is it perceived by practitioners filling most positions that this format in future years will lead to services being

TABLE 7.22

Did ZBB Provide More Services Without Increasing Costs?

| | Participants | | | |
Response	Line Personnel	Departmental Budget Analysts	CAO Budget Analysts	CAO Programmers
Yes	20.0%	37.5%	0.0%	8.3%
Uncertain	4.0	12.5	20.0	33.3
No	76.0	50.0	80.0	58.3
Total	100.0 (25)	100.0 (8)	100.0 (5)	100.0 (12)

Note: X^2 = 9.28673 (P = .158); Cramer's V = .304.
Source: Compiled by the author.

carried out without increasing costs. The exception is found among CAO programmers, who are clearly more optimistic about improving government efficiency than persons occupying other positions (Table 7.23). Thus participants previously utilizing quantitative measures of service performance and objectives in their job tasks differ from others in the belief that cost savings will eventually result through ZBB. The variation among positions with regard to future years is significant at the .01 level, and the Cramer's V is .391.

Zero-base budgeting also has been suggested as a way of providing a better quality of government service. In essence, this budget technique may not bring cost savings, but it could enable governments to deliver more effective services. Tables 7.24 and 7.25 report the feelings they have about the impact of ZBB on the quality of services, and its potential impact in future years. As can be seen in Table 7.24, there is overwhelming agreement that the initial ZBB effort did not lead to a better quality of services. The "no" responses range from 58.3 percent for CAO programmers to 100.0 percent for CAO budget analysts. There is some expectation of ZBB leading in later years to a better quality of services, however, as can be seen in the two tables by comparing the responses of participants holding each position; in all groups the percentage of "yes" responses regarding future years is higher than the percentage of "yes" responses regarding the current year. The largest change occurs with CAO program personnel. This group also tends to be more optimistic than others about ZBB ultimately improving service quality. Line personnel, on the other hand, are the most pessimistic about this point. To some degree, this variation may reflect differences in perspective regarding the use of quantitative indicators to evaluate the extent to which services contribute to the achievement of objectives.

TABLE 7.23

Will ZBB Provide More Services Without Increasing Costs in Later Years?

	Participants			
Response	Line Personnel	Departmental Budget Analysts	Analysts	CAO Programmers
Yes	7.7%	25.0%	20.0%	46.2%
Uncertain	34.6	0.0	0.0	38.5
No	57.7	75.0	80.0	15.4
Total	100.0 (26)	100.0 (8)	100.0 (5)	100.0 (13)

Note: X^2 = 15.93045 (P = .014)*
Cramer's V = .391
*Significant at the .05 level
Source: Compiled by the author.

Zero-base budgeting could also prove beneficial indirectly by improving the quality of management information generated by the budget process. Thus even if the format does not directly result in different choices or more efficient or effective services, it could provide management with better information on which to base decisions outside the budgetary process. As can be seen in Table 7.26, there is some support for this supposition; those feeling ZBB has been bene-

TABLE 7. 24

Did ZBB Provide a Better Quality of Services?

		Participants		
Response	Line Personnel	Departmental Budget Analysts	CAO Budget Analysts	CAO Programmers
Yes	12. 0%	25. 0%	0. 0%	8. 3%
Uncertain	24. 0	12. 5	0. 0	33. 3
No	64. 0	62. 5	100. 0	58. 3
Total	100. 0 (25)	100. 0 (8)	100. 0 (5)	100. 0 (12)

Note: X^2 = 5. 04798 (P = . 538); Cramer's V = . 225.
Source: Compiled by the author.

TABLE 7. 25

Will ZBB Provide Better Services in Future Years?

		Participants		
Response	Line Personnel	Departmental Budget Analysts	CAO Budget Analysts	CAO Programmers
Yes	24. 0%	50. 0%	40. 0%	69. 2%
Uncertain	24. 0	25. 0	40. 0	23. 1
No	52. 0	25. 0	20. 0	7. 7
Total	100. 0 (25)	100. 0 (8)	100. 0 (5)	100. 0 (13)

Note: X^2 = 10. 50499 (P = . 105); Cramer's V = . 321.
Source: Compiled by the author.

ficial vary from 44.0 percent of departmental line personnel to 60.0 percent of CAO budget analysts. It is unclear from this survey as to what specific new information was generated or how it is being put to use. The responses do indicate, however, a belief by many participants in each group that ZBB can be useful in this context.

TABLE 7.26

Impact of ZBB on Quality of Management Information
Compared to Regular Budget System

	Participants			
Response	Line Personnel	Departmental Budget Analysts	CAO Budget Analysts	CAO Programmers
Better quality with ZBB	44.0%	57.1%	60.0%	45.5%
The same or less with ZBB	56.0	42.9	40.0	54.5
Total	100.0 (25)	100.0 (7)	100.0 (5)	100.0 (11)

Note: $X^2 = 0.71167$ (P = .871); Cramer's V = .122.
Source: Compiled by the author.

The areas where differences among groups emerge concern whether or not ZBB will enable the city of New Orleans in the future to provide services that are more cost efficient, and a better quality of services. CAO programmers are the most optimistic about these benefits accruing from the continuation of this process, while line personnel are the most pessimistic. The positive feelings of CAO program developers and evaluators probably stem from the belief that zero-base budgeting can be the vehicle for evaluating programs. It will be possible, in their view, to determine what undertakings are not achieving meaningful results through this budget process. Steps can then be taken to either eliminate these efforts or improve them. Line persons, on the other hand, have little familiarity with the use of quantitative measures relating activities to objectives as a mechanism to pass judgment on the success or failure of programs. Their basic concerns are the daily constraints of service implementation. Given their orientation, it is not surprising that these practitioners clearly are skeptical about ZBB improving government efficiency and effectiveness.

Personal Commitment to Zero-Base Budgeting

The ultimate success or failure of any budget innovation rests on its acceptance by participants filling all roles involved in the budget process. Some insight into which roles might cause ZBB's demise can be obtained by determining the positions where support for this change is weak. Thus a question of interest is whether commitment to zero-base budgeting in New Orleans differs among participants.

A lack of personal commitment would not be surprising, given the difficulties encountered by practitioners, as noted previously. Most CAO programmers, however, could be expected to be committed to this new format despite the problems faced during the initial year. These individuals have a strong desire to base budget choices on the use of quantitative information, and also perceive that ZBB can improve government efficiency and effectiveness. It is unclear as to what to anticipate in regard to practitioners who carry out other functions, but lack of support could be anticipated. The other participants are not oriented to developing and using quantitative indicators in the way demanded by ZBB. Nor are they as convinced as CAO programmers that this format will have tangible benefits for New Orleans.

The levels of personal commitment shown in Table 7.27 indicate overwhelming support for zero-base budgeting only among CAO programmers. In each of the other groups a noticeable number of individuals are committed to ZBB, but a substantial portion also are uncertain or uncommitted. Thus New Orleans is not faced with a situation in which all or most practitioners exhibit little or no commitment; but the city does not have the kind of support likely to be necessary for ultimate success. Approval could grow among the uncertain and the uncommitted as some of the difficulties discussed above are ironed out, and as participants in these other roles become more acquainted with the use of quantitative indicators in decision making. In the end, however, it is likely that these participants are going to have to be convinced of the benefits resulting from zero-base budgeting. It will be difficult to increase personal commitment to this budget innovation unless the costs borne by the participants (for example, time and effort) are offset with a belief that meaningful benefits are obtainable for the city and its departments. [17]

TABLE 7.27

Personal Commitment to ZBB

Response	Line Personnel	Departmental Budget Analysts	CAO Budget Analysts	CAO Programmers
		Participants		
Committed	53. 8%	62. 5%	40. 0%	92. 1%
Uncertain	19. 3	37. 5	20. 0	7. 9
Not committed	26. 9	0. 0	40. 0	0. 0
Total	100. 0 (26)	100. 0 (8)	100. 0 (5)	100. 0 (13)

Note: X^2 = 11. 31929 (P = . 079); Cramer's V = . 364.
Source: Compiled by the author.

CONCLUSION

This study has focused on the effort of the city of New Orleans to institute the initial steps of zero-base budgeting in four departments. It addresses several questions that arise when changes in the budget process are instituted by governments. In terms of difficulties encountered with ZBB, New Orleans is experiencing the same problems occurring in other jurisdictions.

ZBB demands more time and effort on the part of practitioners involved in budget preparation. Both advanced planning done before implementation, and instructions issued to participants are viewed as inadequate. There is also a lack of sufficient information to properly complete a zero-base budget. And a noticeable number of participants believe neither they personally nor key actors understand ZBB procedures.

Overall, most participants believe there is some commitment by top management to this system. The one exception is the large number of persons expressing uncertainty about the former mayor's position. Thus New Orleans is not faced with the problem of practitioners believing city leaders are unsupportive of ZBB.

There is little evidence that zero-base budgeting to date has altered relationships between departments and the central administration. It is perceived, nevertheless, that the potential exists for increasing central administrative leverage over decisions through this budget format. If this eventually proves true, then ZBB will fulfill its promise of making budgets more responsive to the priorities of top officials.

The success or failure of budget innovations ultimately depends upon the personal commitment of those required to implement the effort. New Orleans is not blessed with a vast majority of practitioners supporting zero-base budgeting. A substantial level of commitment does exist, but probably not enough to sustain ZBB in the long run.

The basic variation in viewpoints among the participants in regard to the above points is between CAO programmers and the remainder of the participants. Persons serving in all positions point out that problems surfaced during implementation, but CAO programmers are the most pessimistic about the adequacy of information that is needed to complete a zero-base budget. Yet the same group is the most optimistic about the benefits of ZBB, especially in the long term. These individuals also tend to be more personally committed to this format than other participants.

Program planners and evaluators are acquainted with the difficulties of developing quantitative measures of services performed and objectives achieved. At the same time, they are convinced of the efficacy of the ZBB effort. Program development and evaluation demands the utilization of quantitative indicators and assumes successful development and application of such indicators will lead to beneficial results. In essence, a decision-making process like zero-base budgeting is viewed as having the potential for improving the quality of services; but budget analysts at the departmental and CAO levels have not extensively used quantitative measures. They also tend to be more skeptical about benefits resulting from such a process.

It is impossible, on the basis of this study, to make any predictions about zero-base budgeting becoming a permanent fixture in New Orleans. The city expanded its use to all departments during 1978, thus demonstrating a commitment to its implementation. Its success is likely, in the long run, however, to depend upon practitioners being convinced that the costs of the process in terms of time, effort, and the development of new quantitative indicators, are outweighed by benefits to their departments and the city as a whole. Permanent implementation will remain an open question as long as a substantial number of people serving in given positions question the usefulness of this format. New Orleans and other governments adopting ZBB not only need to work out the inevitable problems, but also must secure the support of each role involved in the budgetary process. If this is not done, zero-base budgeting will probably be only a temporary phenomenon.

NOTES

1. Allen Schick, "The Road to PPB: The Stages of Budget Reform," Public Administration Review 26 (December 1966): 243-58.

2. See, for instance, Donald F. Haider, "Zero Base: Federal Style," Public Administration Review 37 (July/August 1977): 400-7; Michael Granof and Dale A. Kinzel, "Zero Based Budgeting: Modest Proposal for Reform," The Federal Accountant 23 (December 1974): 50-56; Peter A. Phyrr, Zero-Base Budgeting (New York: John Wiley and Sons, 1973); Peter A. Phyrr, "The Zero-Base Approach to Government Budgeting," Public Administration Review 37 (January/February 1977): 1-8; Graeme M. Taylor, "Introduction to Zero-Base Budgeting," The Bureaucrat 6 (Spring 1977): 33-55; and Charlie B. Tyer, "Zero-Base Budgeting: A Critical Analysis," Southern Review of Public Administration 1 (June 1977): 80-107.

3. Roy Lee Hogan, "Zero-Base Budgeting: A Rationalistic Attempt to Improve the Texas Budget System," Unpublished study (Austin: University of Texas, December 1975); George Samuel Minmier, An Evaluation of the Zero-Base Budgeting System in Governmental Institutions, Research Monograph No. 68 (Atlanta: School of Business Administration, Georgia State University, 1975); David W. Singleton, Bruce A. Smith, and James R. Cleveland, "Zero-Base Budgeting in Wilmington, Delaware," Governmental Finances 5 (February 1976): 20-29; and Michael J. Scheiring, "Zero-Based Budgeting in New Jersey," State Government 49 (Summer 1976): 174-79.

4. One reason for the failure of planned program budgeting was lack of support from relevant budget participants. See Allen Schick, "A Death in the Bureaucracy: The Demise of Federal PPB," Public Administration Review 33 (March/April 1973): 146-50; and James E. Frank, "A Framework for Analysis of PPB Success and Causality," Administrative Science Quarterly 18 (December 1973): pp. 538-41.

5. Allen Schick, Budget Innovation In The States (Washington, D.C.: Brookings Institution, 1971), pp. 164-91; and Schick, "The Road to PPB: The Stages of Budget Reform," op. cit., p. 257.

6. City of New Orleans, Council Resolution R-78-25, December 1, 1976.

7. See Phyrr, "The Zero-Base Approach to Government Budgeting," op. cit., p. 8; and Taylor, p. 35.

8. For more about zero-base elements, see Haider, op. cit.; Granof and Kinzel, op. cit.; Phyrr, Zero-Base Budgeting, op. cit.; Taylor, op. cit.; and Tyer, op. cit.

9. City of New Orleans, Program Development and Coordination Division, City of New Orleans, Zero Base Budget Pilot Program

Instructions for Budget Preparation (New Orleans: Chief Administrative Office, July 21, 1977).

10. Ibid., pp. 1-2.

11. Many of the questions were taken from Minmier, An Evaluation of the Zero-Base Budgetary System in Governmental Institutions.

12. See Hogan, op. cit.; Minmier, op. cit.; Singleton, Smith, and Cleveland, op. cit.; and Scheiring, op. cit.

13. Herbert Blalock, Jr., Social Statistics (New York: McGraw-Hill, 1972), pp. 297-98.

14. Frank, op. cit., pp. 539-40.

15. Schick, "The Road to PPB: The Stages of Reform," op. cit., p. 257.

16. See, for instance, Phyrr, "The Zero-Base Approach to Government Budgeting," op. cit.; and Taylor, "Introduction to Zero-Base Budgeting," op. cit.

17. The inability of many practitioners to perceive tangible benefits deriving from planned program budgeting contributed to the demise of this format. See Schick, "The Demise of Federal PPB," op. cit., pp. 148-50.

8

APPLYING ZBB
TO MEET DIVERSE
BUDGETING OBJECTIVES

Douglas H. Wilton
Lewis F. McLain, Jr.
Bruce A. Smith

This study contrasts the experiences of two significantly different local governments in implementing zero-base budgeting (ZBB). The city of Garland, Texas is now completing its fifth annual budget cycle under the zero-base budgeting concept, and the city of Wilmington, Delaware has three years' experience with ZBB. By comparing their experiences, it is possible to illustrate the flexibility of zero-base budgeting in serving widely different budgeting objectives. It is also instructive to examine the year-to-year changes that have taken place in these two applications of the ZBB concept as a practical reflection of the impact made by this currently popular management tool.

THE GARLAND AND WILMINGTON ENVIRONMENTS

It will not be difficult to see the remarkable contrast between the two settings of Garland and Wilmington. Wilmington, Delaware

---

Douglas H. Wilton, CPA, is a partner in the Management Services Division of Touche Ross and Company. He has been directly involved in several ZBB implementation projects for state and local governments. Lewis F. McLain, Jr. is county budget officer for Dallas County, Texas, where he has managed the installation of zero-base budgeting. He was previously budget director for the city of Garland, Texas. Bruce A. Smith, Ph.D., is the management assistant in the Office of the Mayor, in the city of Wilmington, Delaware, where he was instrumental in the initial utilization of ZBB techniques.

is established, urban, and situated in the East Coast megalopolis. Its population and tax base have decreased and are now stagnant. Wilmington operates under the strong mayor-council form of government. The city government work force is unionized. In the mid-1970s, when Wilmington first implemented zero-base budgeting, the city had a discretionary budget of approximately $25 million.

Garland, Texas on the other hand, is a younger, suburban, Sun Belt community with a relatively affluent and stable economic base. The city operates under a streamlined council-manager form of government, which has no municipal union with which to cope. Having reorganized the city government in the early 1970s, Garland's administration had significant experience with advanced management techniques prior to ZBB implementation. It administers a general-fund budget of approximately $20 million.

Both of these municipalities had committed and capable professional personnel carrying out their budget and finance functions. Factors largely beyond their control forced Wilmington to seek a useful means of controlling and limiting its discretionary fiscal activity, while Garland sought an equally useful tool for expanding its budgetary expenditures in an orderly and publicly meaningful way. At the time of their respective zero-base budgeting implementations, both municipalities were convinced of the inadequacy of their existing budget processes, and were committed to improving municipal management and the budget process. Both had general-fund budgets in the low-eight figures. But, although some differences will be observed in their respective methods of applying zero-base budgeting—as we shall discuss—it is particularly interesting to note that both municipalities selected ZBB to support their seemingly opposite budget objectives.

METHODS OF IMPLEMENTATION

Garland and Wilmington were relatively consistent in applying the methodical implementation procedure illustrated in Figure 8.1. It may be instructive to review, in more detail, the procedure by which both municipalities successfully implemented this complex technique that affects broadly and profoundly their respective organizations. The procedures consist of the conceptual activities illustrated in the Figure.

Determination of Strategy

Two strategic courses of action lay before the budget planners for Garland and Wilmington. Each municipality found it could either

FIGURE 8.1

Zero-Base Budgeting: The Implementation Process

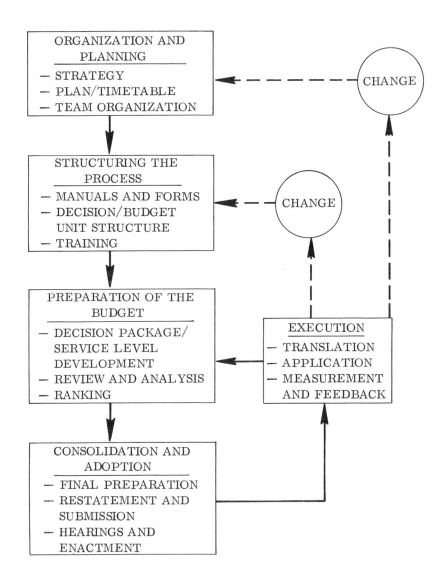

Source: Compiled by the author.

implement ZBB selectively in pilot agencies and programs, or that the new technique could be implemented comprehensively throughout the municipal governments. Both Garland and Wilmington elected to implement on a comprehensive basis. Garland's choice was made, however, after a preliminary test of draft forms and procedures in two agencies.

Development of a Plan and Timetable

Working with budgetary and systems consultants, each municipality laid out a general plan and estimated timetable for the remaining steps in the implementation procedure. Wilmington's planning commenced six months in advance of the budget-approval deadline, while Garland began planning four months prior to budget submission. Subsequent use and refinement of the general plan confirm the need for initial planning as an essential first step in successful implementation. An essential element of this activity is the marshaling of the municipal commitment required to push through a difficult new process in a complex environment, sometimes characterized by a degree of administrative inertia.

Organization of an Implementation Team

In each instance a team of qualified and committed budget professionals was organized to work with the city consultants throughout the implementation process and to lead the budget-preparation effort in future cycles.

Development of Forms and Manuals

Because the process was a complex and new one for both installations, it was necessary to document it and make it orderly through the use of standard forms and procedural guidelines. These materials were prepared internally, but under the guidance of consultants. They utilized the best information available on requirements for initial ZBB implementation. Subsequent budget cycles have seen marked reductions in the volume of forms and paperwork, although each city prepares a new manual for each cycle. Garland has revised its budget forms annually to reflect refinements in the process.

Definition of Decision/Budget Units

As might have been expected, terminology has differed, even within the context of similar procedures. Definition, for budget purposes, of the major subdivisions of the municipalities—called decision units in one case, budget units in the other—constituted the next step in the implementation process. This step has likewise been refined in subsequent budget cycles.

Conduct of Training

The implementation team and other budget personnel were trained to understand the technique and the process thoroughly. In addition, management personnel from all budget/decision units were given a full day of training in zero-base budgeting procedures. Garland followed its group training with one-on-one visits to each agency, in an attempt to draw out and resolve any questions or problems that might have been suppressed during the group sessions. This training, and the forms and manuals previously developed, formed the broad base of confidence from which the overall technique was successfully implemented.

Definition and Development of Service Levels/Decision Packages

Again, terminology differed where substance and procedure were relatively similar. Decision-unit managers, utilizing guidelines developed and furnished centrally, defined the incremental service levels and decision packages, in support of the resources that were being requested through the budget process. In both cities it was necessary to assist some budget/decision unit managers in refining their initially submitted packages to have them reflect adherence to guidelines and meet the overall objectives of zero-base budgeting.

Review and Analysis

Service-level documentation and decision packages were reviewed centrally by the implementation teams and were analyzed by them to confirm the soundness of supporting details and to assist in defining priorities for the subsequent ranking process. The review and analysis in both municipalities concerned not only quantitative and administrative issues but also the political, human, and other subjective factors that so often define the outcome of events in the public sector.

Ranking

Decision packages and service level documentation were then submitted to municipal management to set the citywide priorities for resource allocation. In both instances, departmental priorities were selectively overruled by top management, and instances of budgetary game playing were uncovered and corrected. Similar techniques were used in Garland and Wilmington to separate service levels and decision packages that were obviously of high priority—and, likewise, of low priority—from those requiring serious discretionary action. The ranking process then focused on the discretionary items, again utilizing structured and subjective techniques to reach a consensus as to priorities.

Finalization of Budget

After the final citywide ranking of service levels/decision packages, decision tables were constructed to array potential resource requirements in sequence, and cumulatively, against the estimated resources available to meet these demands. Final adjustment and documentation determined the service levels to be included among those recommended for funding. Garland's budget was then translated into the traditional format required by its charter for submission to its council.

Submission and Enactment

The administrative budgets in both municipalities were then submitted to their legislative bodies for consideration and enactment. The legislative process in both instances effected some changes in the projected expenditure levels and relative priorities developed through the zero-base budgeting technique.

INITIAL CONTRASTS

Aside from the differences in terminology and detailed procedures, perhaps the most remarkable contrast between Garland's and Wilmington's implementation experience was the difference in the guidelines used by decision-unit managers for the development of their service levels and decision packages. Garland's initial guidelines required managers to identify the level of service that would be provided under the most severe budgetary circumstances. These guidelines broke down in practice, however, somewhat affecting the credibility of the ZBB process. In most decision units, the "minimum level" was identified and developed, but no decision units were actually funded for less than the current level of service, because to have done so would have been unrealistic. Wilmington's guidelines stipulated 40 percent to 60 percent of the existing level of expenditures as the target for the minimum service level within a budget unit. The guidelines used reflect the contrasting objectives of the two municipalities—namely, the orderly expansion of budgetary expenditures in Garland, and the reduction and control of these expenditures in Wilmington. It is interesting to note that in its second and third ZBB years, Wilmington utilized the concept of scaled reductions from the existing level of expenditures, rather than stipulating a minimum service level from which to expand incrementally.

Garland's initial cycle saw an attempt to define decision units in a way which crossed functional lines—in at least one instance—and thereby confused accountability aspects of the process. In subsequent cycles this practice has been eliminated. Budget-unit definitions have consistently followed organizational lines in Wilmington.

Another interesting contrast is the format utilized for presentation to the council. Wilmington utilized the zero-base budgeting format in presenting its budget to the City Council, since members of the council had been involved in the ZBB development process. The process of council hearings and enactment saw fewer department-head attempts to exert political pressure and circumvent the explicit priorities established by the ZBB process than had occurred under the implicit priorities established by the incremental process. Several council members, furthermore, showed at least the normal level of interest in budgeted expenditures for specific items, rather than in the service levels and performance measures that were intended to focus legislative interest on areas of greater substance.

Garland's council also exhibited the traditional interest in specific line items. This, however, is not surprising, since Garland's budget was presented in the traditional format in order to satisfy the requirements of its city charter. The one attempt to use only ZBB formats in the proposed budget was not repeated, because the council members demanded greater detail in order to demonstrate to constituents their scrutiny of municipal spending. Zero-base budgeting data on all decision packages and performance measures were provided in support of the line-item budget.

In neither environment does the ZBB technique itself appear to have been a political factor. This is not to say, however, that ZBB served to suppress the political characteristics of the respective public bodies. Indeed—although it is not necessarily attributable to the budget process—the council and administration in Garland had grown to be so at odds late in 1977 that the city manager and several other administration officials resigned or were dismissed.

SUBSEQUENT CHANGES

The city of Garland has continued to refine the zero-base budgeting process as initially implemented. Among the refinements implemented is an increase in detail support for specific lines—such as vehicles—within decision packages. This reflects the council's continuing interest in assuring adequate support for politically sensitive line items. A better crosswalk has been established between zero-base budgeting formats and the accounting structure of the city. Decision units are now better related to traditional budget accounts. Second- and third-year cycles saw strict correspondence between decision units and function codes; and more recent cycles have broken down each function into its constituent programs for decision-unit purposes. There have been simplifications in the systems and procedures of the ZBB process. Garland appears to be moving toward more selective application of zero-base budgeting, rather than the annual comprehensive application that has been used. These and other changes have required the preparation of an elaborate new budget manual on an annual basis.

Wilmington's subsequent cycles have focused on simplifying the process and reducing paperwork. As we have noted, the guidelines for service levels issued to budget-unit heads in the first ZBB cycle required the specification of the current level of service and expenditure, along with a first and second reduction from the current level as well as an optional expansion of service and expenditure. The second cycle in Wilmington saw increased emphasis on the development of program/performance measures, which reflects a growing facility with the more mechanical aspects of ZBB as well as a trend toward more meaningful operational data in the budget process. The third cycle saw increased emphasis on long-range planning through the development of a second-year budget plan, which will be reviewed in conjunction with the next budget cycle.

Wilmington's administration operates under an informal management-by-objectives program, which was more thoroughly integrated with the ZBB process during the second and third budget cycles. In addition, the process of ranking service levels on a citywide basis saw broadened participation by municipal officials, including budget-unit directors. Accordingly, during administrative hearings, the level of emphasis on service levels and performance measures was relatively greater with respect to projected expenditures than it had been in Wilmington's initial ZBB cycle.

PROBABLE IMPACT

Since the implementation of zero-base budgeting, Wilmington points to the achievement of constant-dollar budgetary expenditure reductions on an overall basis. This remarkable achievement has been attributed in large measure to the use of zero-base budgeting techniques. Although municipal officials continue to have difficulty in defining and gathering meaningful performance measures, Wilmington is generally satisfied with the zero-base budgeting installation, and continues to use the technique in spite of its incremental administrative workload.

Garland's administration has been satisfied with the results it has achieved through the use of zero-base budgeting. In fact, the concept has been expanded to apply to the assignment of priorities for general revenue-sharing projects. As noted, the city has also expanded the application of ZBB from the general activity level to the more detailed program level. Garland's recent efforts have continued the refinement initiated earlier in the concept of minimum service levels. The base-level decision package has thus evolved through the following concepts in succeeding budget cycles: a very severe minimum level, a total dollar amount of the prior year's budget, a reduction of at least one program per function, and a current level. This may not sound much like conventional ZBB wisdom—but it works in practice, because it fits the user's budgeting objectives. In general, although the technique is no panacea, nor even the central feature of advanced management in Garland, municipal officials have accepted ZBB as an important aspect of their overall management process, and Garland's new administration is continuing to use ZBB in its general form.

CONCLUSIONS

One might generalize from these observations and draw the following conclusions concerning the use of zero-base budgeting in the municipal government setting:

1. The use of the ZBB technique will require more work of line managers in the budgetary process.
2. Increased management involvement in budget decisions will place additional demands on many officials, but will improve the quality and acceptance of the budget process.
3. Some organizational impact, in terms of divisional reorganizations to fit budget-unit structures, will inevitably emerge where ZBB has been implemented. Because of expanded participation, analysis,

and support, ZBB will enhance the credibility of almost any budget process.

4. The implementation of zero-base budgeting will provide the opportunity for meaningful involvement of the legislative branch in the development and enactment of the budget. The ZBB process facilitates—indeed, requires—the integration of activities for budgeting and planning purposes, regardless of the funding sources (federal, local, state, other) intended to support the planned activities.

5. Zero-base budgeting inevitably leads to improved quality in budget decisions as to program priorities, performance measures, and expenditure levels, through vastly improved management involvement and dialogue in the budgetary process.

In spite of the controversy and general difficulty that have surrounded ZBB wherever it has gone, the installations in Wilmington and Garland must be termed successful by any standard. It seems apparent that some form of zero-base budgeting will continue to be utilized in these two municipalities, which have such widely different characteristics and budgeting objectives, because ZBB has proven useful.

9

ZERO-BASE BUDGETING IN NEW MEXICO

John D. LaFaver

The Legislative Finance Committee (LFC), a permanent, joint, interim committee of the New Mexico Legislature, is mandated by statute to annually submit an independent state budget recommendation to the Legislature. (The committee's first legislative budget was presented in 1970.) In fulfilling this mandate, the committee begins public hearings in late September which continue to early December. Approximately 200 hours of hearings are held during this period. The resulting budget, embodying recommendations for funding all state agencies and public schools, is then submitted to the Legislature in January.

EARLY BUDGET PROBLEMS

The committee and its staff, after the initial budget presentation in 1970, were dissatisfied with the appropriating-budgeting process in several respects.

1. There was little emphasis placed on activities or programs previously funded. Most effort was expended in analyzing requests for additional appropriations.

———————————

John D. LaFaver is a senior staff member of the Legislative Finance Committee in New Mexico. The views expresses are Mr. LaFaver's and are not neccessarily those of the Legislative Finance Committee.

Reprinted with permission from <u>State Government</u>, Spring, 1974.

2. Little information was available concerning the public services to be provided with given appropriations.

3. In most instances, legislative committees exerted little effort in clarifying their intent of how money should be spent and what performance results would be anticipated.

4. The system failed to elicit funding alternatives and priorities from agencies. For a variety of reasons, agencies seldom receive an appropriation in the amount requested. If meaningful alternatives are not presented to the Legislature, that body is handicapped in making rational appropriations.

5. When appropriations were less than requests, and when the Legislature failed to express its intent as to what programs or projects were included within appropriations, agencies often made the same requests year after year—even though legislative staff, at least, thought the requests had been funded. Agencies also sought and received federal funding for projects funded from the state general fund.

THE EARLY ZERO-BASE BUDGETING

In an attempt to address some of these concerns, the LFC requested 10 executive agencies to justify their programs and budget requests to the 1971 Legislature as though they were requesting an appropriation for the first time. Because of this "starting-from-scratch" approach, the concept was labeled "zero-base" budgeting.

The selected agencies represented a relatively insignificant portion of state government. (Appropriation to these agencies constituted about 1 percent of the total state general fund appropriation.) The agencies were not selected randomly. Those chosen were generally controversial and thought to be in need of thorough scrutiny.

The LFC recommended the abolishment of three of the 10 agencies; the programs of two were recommended to be substantially restructured; and the remaining five received "business as usual" analyses and recommendations.

The recommendations for abolishing the three agencies met with difficulty in the first legislative session of a new administration. The inclination was to give a newly elected Governor the opportunity to improve performance records. However, one agency was abolished and another substantially reorganized.

While the initial effort was but a small and shaky first step at budget reform, several important lessons were learned.

1. It simply was not reasonable to expect an agency to routinely furnish information that might result in a lower appropriation—no matter what the justification might be.

2. Since the State's fiscal outlook was optimistic, there was little impetus to cut budgets or eliminate marginal programs. Thus, a budget system designed to locate duplication and thus reduce budgets was out of phase in a period of increasing revenues.

3. The best committee analyses were often of agencies making the least effort in their budget presentations. When agencies often failed to address the critical issues of their programs, the LFC and its staff attempted to define and research the issues. An independent research staff was essential.

4. Several agencies not submitting zero-base budgets were recommended to be significantly restructured as a result of "routine" analyses. Of course, analysts applying a "starting-from-scratch" approach to a few selected agencies found it difficult to turn that approach off when analyzing other agencies. The resultant change in viewpoint led to the challenging of several obsolete, but heretofore unquestioned, programs. The Legislature accepted many of these recommendations.

THE "70 PERCENT" ZERO-BASE

While the committee's initial experiment at budget innovation had only nominal impact on the appropriating process during the 1971 Legislature, the LFC determined to continue its efforts. What eventually evolved was a compromise between a "comprehensive" and an "incremental" budget request (i.e., between a "starting-from-scratch" budget and taking last year's budget for granted).

Essential to the new zero-base approach was the "level of effort" concept by which agency managers would detail what could and could not be accomplished at several funding levels. The budget, which would interface to the customary line-item format (which the executive budget division continued to require), would be presented in "decision packages." These packages were determined by, first, separating each agency into several quasi-independent units that could be readily identified and analyzed and, second, establishing several levels of effort for each unit. The levels suggested were 70 percent of current budget, 95-100 percent of current budget, and separate units for each major request above current budget. The manager would state for each funding level what performance levels could be expected. Major requests for new funding that involved several units within a department (e.g., a general personnel upgrading) would be set out as separate decision packages. All decision packages then would compete against each other and would finally be ranked in priority order. In effect, an agency's legislative budget request was a "shopping list" that the Legislature could fund at its discretion based, hopefully, on certain performance criteria as well as dollars available.

Sixteen agencies were requested to submit their budget requests on the new zero-base format. Several larger agencies were chosen, but the appropriation to those selected still represented only about 4 percent of the total state general fund appropriation.

The effort in preparing for the 1972 Legislature represented a departure from the previous effort in several respects.

1. In turning away from a "starting-from-scratch" or comprehensive budget review, the LFC realized that abolishment of an agency, no matter what its performance record might be, is always difficult and usually impossible.

2. A budget addressed to justifying an agency's existence does not examine the critical issue facing a finance committee—that of how much should be allocated. Particularly in the large agencies, there is no real question but that the agencies will continue to operate. The question is, "At what level?"

3. In allocating significant portions of staff time to format design and in educating agency personnel in the use of the new forms, the committee believed that the agencies, to some degree, could analyze themselves—thus, making LFC staff time more productive.

4. The need for substantially more program performance information necessitated the involvement of significantly more agency personnel. No longer could the budget be the mysterious product of the accounting section.

The LFC, while realizing that the product could be improved, was optimistic in its 1972 presentation. The legislative budget stated, "When the zero-base budget is well prepared, it provides the Legislature with an excellent basis for making policy judgments. The committee is convinced that zero-base budgeting is feasible given competent administration within state agencies coupled with a willingness to undertake a new approach. Conversely, the technique quickly indicates those agencies where these qualities are lacking."

After the 1972 session, the LFC sponsored a joint meeting with the standing finance committees to evaluate the impact and determine the future of zero-base. The view which emerged was that the system should be continued and expanded. Finance committee members expressed the need for more and better financial information based on services to be purchased.

THE 1973 EFFORT

Some 35 agencies were requested to submit zero-base budgets prior to the 1973 Legislature. Those 35 represented a significant increase in state funding from previous years. (Total expenditures of the 35 accounted for just over 40 percent of total state expense, including federal and earmarked funds.) The major areas not included in the effort were higher education (25 percent of state spending) and public schools (26 percent of state funding). The significant increase in the number and size of agencies participating placed a tremendous load on committee staff.

The format was significantly altered from that of 1972, with the aim of reducing the narrative and increasing the volume of quantitative performance information. The revised format also used a more sophisticated (and more complex) process for determining the levels of effort. Some terminology was changed. But the end result—that of presenting the Legislature with alternative funding levels tied to performance commitments—was unchanged.

The new system was explained to a joint meeting of the standing finance committees just prior to the session and enthusiasm was expressed for tying performance commitments to dollars appropriated. While the committees had some difficulty in fully utilizing the new system under the press of business, significant support was apparent. A joint memorial was unanimously passed which called for the implementation of an executive zero-base budget for presentation to the 1974 Legislature.

RECENT MODIFICATIONS

In preparing for the 1974 Legislature, the legislative and executive budget staffs agreed to a single budget format—thus eliminating the dual agency presentations of previous years. As a result, agency workload in budget preparation was reduced, and the debate of significant budget issues was sharpened.

The new format continued to incorporate a modified "level of effort" concept. The major modification was the abandonment of the level of effort below the present base. Thus, a rigidly defined base was the first level of effort and expansion items only were ranked in priority order. Performance commitments continued to be required of each level of effort including the base. While the new format did not require agency performance commitments at lower than the base level, some analyses concluded that base level performance commitments could, in effect, be accomplished at lower cost than requested.

While it might be argued that the 1974 modification was a further step away from true zero-base analysis, the step was taken primarily in response to the State's fiscal situation. Some were predicting a surplus as high as $100 million or nearly 30 percent of the present general fund budget. With such optimistic forecasts, it was obvious that the decision range for most budgets would be between 110 and 120 percent of present appropriations. Thus, there seemed to be little point in developing a 70 percent budget. In future years, the decision range should be altered annually depending on projected revenues.

Since it was obvious that appropriations to most agencies would increase significantly, obtaining higher performance commitments was extremely important. Whether meaningful commitments were indeed made, of course, remains to be seen. Complicating the matter is the fact that a new administration will take office prior to the next legislative session, and commitments made by outgoing administrators may tend to get lost in the shuffle. An important job of the Legislature and its staff should be to insure that new executive managers are aware that certain commitments have been made and will be monitored. At the same time, a new executive should be given flexibility to seek new directions and reorder old priorities.

EVALUATION OF THE CONCEPT

Because program managers are likely to judge a new budgeting system by the increased appropriation received and legislators and staff usually evaluate on the opposite basis, no consensus is likely on the success of zero-base in New Mexico. Even though appropriations have increased significantly since the inception of zero-base, legislators continue to support budget innovation. However, agency managers often feel uncomfortable with such close legislative scrutiny.

States considering innovative techniques in budgeting—particularly where the Legislature is providing the impetus in demanding change—should expect to face some of the same problems faced in New Mexico. The problem areas presented below are compiled from agency critiques and staff observations with the aim of eliminating the plowing of already-tilled ground in other States.

1. Agency preparation of two budget documents (one for the Legislature and one for the executive) should be avoided if possible.

2. The part-time nature of most Legislatures, as well as the turnover in finance committees, frustrate efforts at educating the lawmakers in the need for budget reform. Even the most conscientious members of standing finance committees have little time to understand the subtleties of a new budgeting system under the press of business. Often the most that can be hoped for is for the legislators to utilize available staff expertise. However, in 30- or 60-day legislative sessions as New Mexico has, time often does not permit the debate of even major budget issues.

3. A competent budget presentation often raises more issues than are answered. It is not reasonable to expect a set of forms to enable an agency to analyze itself to the satisfaction of a critical analyst. As such, significant portions of time need to be reserved for independent examination. New forms usually increase rather than reduce the need for such analysis.

4. Zero-base budgeting will not deter agencies from including unjustifiable cost increases in the decision package costing. The elimination of these pads through legislative scrutiny offers the agency the excuse that performance commitments no longer are applicable because the appropriation request was altered.

5. Historic cost and performance data are seldom available by the decision unit. As such, estimates usually must be used with the understanding that pertinent data will begin to be compiled for future use.

6. The idea of a 70 percent initial funding level is threatening to many agency personnel. There is a feeling that to even submit a cost figure on such a reduced operation encourages a Legislature to reduce an appropriation.

7. Small (under $200,000 expenditure), highly specialized agencies with very specific statutory mandates are seldom good candidates for a level of effort approach. However, even these agencies should be able to make certain performance commitments.

8. Agencies may attempt to manipulate priority listings by ranking popular items lower than items that otherwise would have little chance of funding. This "stalking-horse" approach necessitates the alteration of priorities during legislative budget review which leads to agency complaints that their priorities are ignored.

9. Budget preparation time needs to be substantially lengthened during the implementation of a new system. The three months allowed in New Mexico was felt inadequate.

10. Agencies operating with several sources of earmarked funds (usually federal grants), find it difficult to rank program priorities. Federal grants requiring little or no state participation are difficult to refuse no matter what their purpose.

11. Proprietory agencies (those that earn operating income) find the level of effort approach difficult to apply to their operation. Functions such as university food services or prison industries, if not subsidized, base their operating level solely on demand for their product. This demand is expressed through direct payment for services rendered rather than through the indirect process of taxation and appropriation. However, most agencies operating on "earmarked" revenues are not proprietory and can effectively utilize the zero-base approach.

12. Without a great deal of care, performance measures often show how busy people are rather than the cost-benefit of their activity.

13. Zero-base makes the decision process more explicit and open to scrutiny. Some agencies will see this openness as a threat to manager flexibility, while others view it as a valuable managerial tool.

14. The involvement of program managers in the budget preparation process is one of the significant strengths of zero-base budgeting.

The construction of a budget is too important to be left to agency accountants.

15. The involvement of legislative staff in assisting executive agencies with budget innovation risks compromising an independent analysis of executive proposals. However, the choice may be whether to have innovation or not.

CONCLUSION

The improvements to New Mexico state government occasioned by zero-base budgeting are neither as great as originally anticipated nor as minimal as detractors would claim. The concept that a previous funding level does not, in itself, justify future funding is not yet totally accepted. Several years of accelerating increases in tax revenues have scarcely encouraged a critical analysis of current spending levels.

However, without a budget system that continually forces the reevaluation of program performance, there is little incentive for governmental agencies to either improve their operation or economize in the use of public funds.

10

A LOOK AT
ZERO-BASE BUDGETING—
THE GEORGIA EXPERIENCE

George S. Minmier
Roger H. Hermanson

In November 1970 Jimmy Carter was elected governor of the state of Georgia. Mr. Carter had campaigned on the central issue of reorganization of the Executive Branch of Georgia's government, and he began making plans for reorganization immediately after being elected. During his research, he discovered an article by Peter Phyrr in the November-December 1970 issue of the Harvard Business Review describing the zero-base budgeting system implemented by Texas Instruments, Inc. [1] His interest in this subject caused him to invite Mr. Phyrr to Atlanta in February 1971 to discuss the feasibility of installing this system in the state government of Georgia.

As a result of this meeting between Governor Carter and Mr. Phyrr, the decision was reached to implement zero-base budgeting in the state government of Georgia for the fiscal year 1972-1973. Mr. Phyrr was offered and accepted a temporary position as consultant to the Bureau of the Budget.

On January 11, 1972, Governor Carter introduced the new zero-base budgeting system in his State of the State Address to the General Assembly of Georgia. [2] In doing so, he stated: "It gives us a unique zero-base budgeting procedure which is almost certain to be copied throughout the Nation." [3]

Dr. Minmier is Assistant Professor of Accounting and Dr. Hermanson is Professor of Accounting, School of Business Administration, Georgia State University.

Reprinted with permission from Atlanta Economic Review, July-August 1976.

In his Budget Address to the Joint Session of the General Assembly of Georgia on January 13, 1972, Governor Carter credited the early implementation of his reorganization study and the new zero-base budget for cutting the spending plans for the current year by $55 million. [4] He further reported that these cuts were made with no significant decrease in state services. In referring to zero-base budgeting, Governor Carter made the following remarks:

"Zero-base budgeting requires every agency in state government to identify each function it performs and the personnel and cost to the taxpayers for performing that function. . . .

"The intense analysis which goes into the construction of a decision package begins at a low level of management within an agency. Constant review and refinement take place at each succeeding level. Each agency assigns a priority to all of its decision packages, and this information is utilized in the allocation of funds in the budget. . . .

"By requiring department heads and their subordinates to take a close look at what they could do with less money, zero-base budgeting encourages the search for more efficient ways to do the job.

"By requiring clear descriptions of the results to be expected from every dollar spent, zero-base budgeting makes it possible to evaluate the performance of an agency against its budget. . . .

"As a result of these techniques we have a budget based on cost analysis and priority ranking. We have a budget in which justification for every dollar was required—for old programs as well as new."[5]

Prior to the change to the zero-base budgeting system, Georgia had used an incremental budgeting system. The basic difference between these systems is that under the incremental approach the prior year's budget is the starting point in developing the next year's budget, but under the zero-base system the planners start from "zero." This means that merely because an item was included in last year's budget does not mean it will appear in the budget for the following year.

Incremental Budgeting

Incremental budgeting is an extension of the theory of incrementalism, which refers to making changes in small bits or increments. As applied to budgeting, incrementalism suggests that attention be directed toward the changes or marginal differences that occur between existing appropriations and proposed expenditures. [6] Such a process accepts the existing base and examines only the increments which extend the current budgeting program into the future. This procedure causes the curve of government activities to be continuous with few zigzags or breaks.

Incremental analysis is an extension of the theory of incrementa budgeting. It was developed by Charles E. Lindblom. Under this approach, the task of deciding is simplified in a number of ways. Rather than being concerned with everything, the decision maker deals with:

1. only that limited set of policy alternatives that are politically relevant, those typically being policies only incrementally different from existing policies;

2. analysis of only those aspects of policies with respect to which the alternatives differ;

3. a view of the policy choice or one in a succession of choices;

4. the marginal values of various social objectives and constraints;

5. an intermixture of evaluation and empirical analysis rather than an empirical analysis of the consequences of policies for objectives independently determined; and

6. only a small number out of all the important relevant values. [7]

Zero-Base Budgeting

In this study the term "zero-base budgeting" refers to a highly structured and systematic budgeting system as developed by Texas Instruments, Inc. , and as applied in the state of Georgia 1972-1973 fiscal year's budget. Within this context, zero-base budgeting is defined as:

"An operating planning and budgeting process which requires each manager to justify his entire budget request in detail, and shifts the burden of proof to each manager to justify why he should spend any money. This procedure requires that all activities and operations be identified in decision packages which will be evaluated and ranked in order of importance by systematic analysis. "[8]

The predominant theory of budgeting applied now, as in the past, is some form of incremental budgeting. It is significant to note that in recent years there have been indications that many administrators are becoming dissatisfied with this traditional theory of incremental budgeting, as evidenced by their recommendations to change to a zero-base approach in solving budget allocation problems. In a 1961 appearance before a United States Senate Subcommittee, Maurice Stans, Budget Director under President Eisenhower, stated: "Every item in a budget ought to be on trial for its life each year and matched against all the other claimants to our resources. "[9]

Zero-base budgeting is especially adaptable to discretionary cost areas in which service and support are the primary outputs. It is this characteristic of zero-base budgeting that has attracted the interest of governmental officials, as most expenditures of government can be classified as discretionary in nature.

METHODOLOGY

To determine the degree of success of the change in the budgeting system used in Georgia an empirical study was made. The following steps were taken in the investigation:

1. Preliminary interviews were held with selected departmental budget analysts to identify topic areas for inclusion in a questionnaire.

2. A questionnaire was prepared and distributed to all 39 budgeting analysts who were using the zero-base system.

3. Follow-up interviews were conducted with selected departmental budget analysts based on their responses to the questionnaire.

4. Interviews were held with selected department heads and with former Governor Jimmy Carter.

5. A detailed examination was made of the zero-base budgeting procedures presently employed.

6. The executive budgets for the state of Georgia were reviewed for the fiscal years 1972, 1973, and 1974.

Of the 39 questionnaires, 32 were returned—a response rate of 82 percent.

For convenience in examining the acceptability or unacceptability of the zero-base budgeting system, two levels of management are distinguished: top management and middle management. Top management consists of the governor and department heads. Middle management consists of budgeting personnel at lower organizational levels within the departments. In addition to the two levels of management mentioned, the attitudes of the budget analysts in the Department of Planning and Budget concerning the zero-based budgeting system were sought.

The Office of Planning and Budget (OPB) is the staff department charged with the responsibility of ensuring that departments comply with the state's budget directives. In addition, staff budget analysts assist the departments with their budget preparation.

TOP MANAGEMENT'S REACTIONS

The zero-base budgeting system had the full support of Governor Carter. This is evidenced by his statementiin an interview conducted on January 7, 1974: "I think our zero-base budgeting system is great for management's decision-making. . . . Zero-base budgeting, in itself, has given me an extremely valuable method by which I can understand what happens deep in a department."[10]

Mr. Carter also was very pleased with the ability of the zero-base budgeting system to provide relevant management information, stating that in his opinion the new budget system's greatest contribution had been in the area of improved management information. An example of the contribution of zero-base budgeting in this area was given by Mr. Carter during the interview. He stated:

"Because of zero-base budgeting we were able to determine that seven different agencies had the responsibility for the education of deaf children. When we broke down the 11,000 or so decision packages and put a computer number on each kind of function, those functions were very quickly identified as being duplicated."[11]

However, Mr. Carter's strong support of the zero-base budgeting system was not shared by some of the department heads. Of 13 department heads interviewed during this survey, only two indicated strong support for the zero-base budgeting system. The other department heads expressed varying degrees of dissatisfaction with this new budgeting system.

Of the 13 department heads who were interviewed, only two (15 percent) expressed the opinion that there may have been some reallocation of financial resources as a result of information supplied to Mr. Carter by the new budgeting system during the reorganization of the Executive Branch of the state. However, they were unable to give a single instance in which the new budgeting system had reallocated resources in their own departments. The other 11 department heads (85 percent) indicated there had been no apparent reallocation of financial resources in their departments as a result of implementing zero-base budgeting.

Mr. Carter expressed a different opinion regarding the contribution of zero-base budgeting in reallocating financial resources in the state. In doing so, he said that he understood the negative responses of the department heads and departmental budget analysts on this issue since the contribution of the new budgeting system in this particular area would not be apparent to them. This was because the reallocation of financial resources was a result of a combination of two factors: (1) the reorganization of the Executive Branch of state government and (2) the manner in which the zero-base budgeting system was initially adopted and implemented.[12]

It is public knowledge in Georgia that there was a substantial reallocation of financial resources within state government during Mr. Carter's administration—especially during his first year in office. However, it was the Executive Reorganization Act of 1972 that has been credited with reallocating the state's financial resources during this period. The purpose of this act was to consolidate under a single authority similar state functions and programs that were previously controlled by different departments and activities throughout state government.

Mr. Carter agreed that it was the Executive Reorganization Act of 1972 that was the primary force in reallocating financial resources within the state. However, he also stated:

"The detection of need for consolidating similar functions within state government is made from the zero-base budgeting technique. It would have been virtually impossible to have made the change we did under the old incremental budgeting system. We have had such a profound change in the structure of government that most people attribute this shifting of roles and also shifting of resources to the reorganization itself which has been so much more present in our mind than to zero-base budgeting."[13]

Much of the dissatisfaction expressed by department heads with zero-base budgeting appeared to result from the way in which it was originally presented and later implemented. Only after the decision had been made to implement the new budgeting system did Mr. Carter hold a series of meetings with his department heads to explain the system and the reasons for its adoption. The fact that the department heads had no input into the original decision to adopt the zero-base budgeting system seemed to have a detrimental effect on their attitudes toward the system.

BUDGET ANALYSTS' REACTIONS

Responses of departmental budget analysts regarding their perceptions of a number of areas were obtained.

Perceived Time, Effort, and Involvement Required Under New System

As would be expected, the time and effort required to convert from the incremental system to the zero-base budgeting system was perceived as being considerable (see Table 10.1). After the initial implementation the time and effort was still perceived as being greater than under the incremental budgeting system (see Table 10.1).

One of the goals of a zero-base budgeting system is to achieve greater involvement of line personnel in the budgeting process. Table 10.1, shows that about 52 percent of the budget analysts believed that department heads became more involved than under the former incremental system. It shows that about 68 percent believed that first-line supervisors became more involved. Only one respondent indicated that there was less involvement by these persons. The OPB budget analysts perceived greater involvement by both agency heads and first-line supervisors than did the departmental analysts.

TABLE 10.1

Perceptions of Budget Analysts Regarding Time, Effort, and Involvement Required Under Zero-Base Budgeting (Segregated as to Departmental Budget Analysts and Analysts in the Office of Planning and Budget)

	Departmental Budget Analysts		OPB Budget Analysts		Total	
	No.	Percent	No.	Percent	No.	Percent
What effect did the zero-base budgeting system have on the time and effort spent in budgeting preparation during the first year of its implementation?						
Increased considerably.	18	78.3	7	87.5	25	80.6
Increased slightly.	5	21.7	1	12.5	6	19.4
Remained about the same.						
Decreased slightly.						
Decreased considerably.						
Now that the zero-based budgeting system has been implemented, how great is the time and effort spent in budget preparation in comparison to the previous incremental budgeting system?						
Much greater.	10	43.5	3	37.5	13	41.9
Slightly more.	7	30.4	4	50.0	11	35.5
About the same.	5	21.7			5	16.1
Slightly less.	1	4.4	1	12.5	2	6.5
Much less						

Did the agency head become more involved in budget formulation after the implementation of zero-base budgeting?

	N	%	N	%	N	%
Much more involved.	5	21.7	4	50.0	9	29.0
Slightly more involved.	5	21.7	2	25.0	7	22.6
About the same.	13	56.6	1	12.5	14	45.2
Slightly less involved.						
Much less involved.			1	12.5	1	3.2

Did first-line supervisors become more involved in budget formulation after the implementation of zero-base budgeting?

	N	%	N	%	N	%
Much more involved.	10	43.5	6	75.0	16	51.6
Slightly more involved.	4	17.4	1	12.5	5	16.1
About the same as before.	9	39.1			9	29.0
Slightly less involved.						
Much less involved.			1	12.5	1	3.2

Source: Compiled by the authors.

TABLE 10.2

Perceptions of Budget Analysts Regarding Adequacy of Planning, Instructions, and Cost Data

	Departmental Budget Analysts		OPB Budget Analysts		Total	
	No.	Percent	No.	Percent	No.	Percent
Do you feel adequate advanced planning on the part of the Budget Bureau was conducted before implementation of the new zero-base budgeting system?						
Yes.	4	17.4	4	44.5	8	25.0
No.	15	65.2	2	22.2	17	53.1
Uncertain.	4	17.4	3	33.3	7	21.9
Do you feel you received adequate instructions during the first year of zero-base budgeting to properly prepare your budget requests?						
Yes.	11	47.8	5	62.5	16	51.6
No.	10	43.5	1	12.5	11	35.5
Uncertain.	2	8.7	2	25.0	4	12.9

	No.	%	No.	%	No.	%
Do you feel you presently have adequate instructions as to how to properly prepare a zero-base budget?						
Yes.	19	82.6	8	88.9	27	84.4
No.	3	13.0	1	11.1	3	9.4
Uncertain.	1	4.4			2	6.2
During the first year of operating with the zero-base budgeting system, did you have adequate cost data available to properly prepare decision packages?						
Yes.	7	30.4	2	25.0	9	29.0
No.	15	65.2	6	75.0	21	67.7
Uncertain.	1	4.4			1	3.2
Do you feel you presently have adequate cost data necessary to properly pre-pare a decision package?						
Yes.	15	65.2	5	55.6	20	62.5
No.	7	30.4	3	33.3	10	31.2
Uncertain.	1	4.4	1	11.1	2	6.3

<u>Source</u>: Compiled by the authors.

161

Adequacy of Planning, Instructions, and Cost Data

The results shown in Table 10.2 indicate that 53 percent of the total respondents believed that the advanced planning was inadequate. Of the departmental analysts, 65 percent believed that advanced planning was inadequate, contrasted to only 22 percent of the OPB analysts who felt this way. Typical comments from departmental analysts were: "The system was designed for industry and not state government." "Each agency should have had time to work with the system to test it before it was implemented."

Although 36 percent of the respondents believed the instructions received during the first year were inadequate, only 9 percent believed they were inadequate after that period. Again, there was more dissatisfaction on the part of departmental analysts than by OPB analysts.

After the implementation of zero-base budgeting, it became apparent that budgeting guidelines were necessary to permit the budgetary process to proceed smoothly. Thus implementation of the zero-base system resulted in the creation of a planning phase prior to the preparation of the budget. Under the former incremental system the planning phase and budgeting phase were conducted concurrently. This change is seen as one of the advantages of adopting the new system.

Regarding cost data, 68 percent believed that adequate cost data were unavailable during the first year; 31 percent believed such cost data were unavailable after that period. It seems that problems with instructions and cost data were severe initially, but in time these problems were being resolved.

Quality of Management Information

One of the proposed benefits accruing from the use of a zero-base budgeting system is an increase in the quality of management information. The quality of management information under the new budgeting system as perceived by budget analysts is presented in Table 10.3. Over half of the analysts (68 percent) indicated an improvement in the quality of management information. The degree of improvement was perceived as being much greater by the OPB budget analysts than by the departmental budget analysts.

Reallocation of Financial Resources

Another proposed benefit accruing from the installation of a zero-base budgeting system is that it would achieve a more efficient allocation of the state's financial resources. The effectiveness of zero-

TABLE 10.3

Quality of Management Information as Perceived by Budget Analysts

	Departmental Budget Analysts		OPB Budget Analysts		Total	
	No.	Percent	No.	Percent	No.	Percent
All good budgeting systems generate information for management planning and control. What effect did the zero-base budgeting system have on the quality of management information as compared to the previous incremental budgeting system?						
Quality of management information substantially improved.	3	13.1	4	50.0	7	22.6
Quality of management information slightly improved.	11	47.8	3	37.5	14	45.2
About the same as before.	9	39.1	1	12.5	10	32.2
Quality of management information slightly decreased.						
Quality of management information substantially decreased.						

Source: Compiled by the authors.

base budgeting in reallocating financial resources as perceived by budget analysts is shown in Table 10.4. Only 7 percent perceived some shifting of financial resources as a result of the use of the new system.

In theory, zero-base budgeting should result in the immediate adjustment of the budget to changes in the level of funding. This is accomplished by preparing a decision-package ranking which lists all decision packages in order of their priority. After a level of funding is established, a cutoff line is employed to divide the decision packages between those to be approved and those to be disapproved. Any subsequent change in the level of funding should require only a shift in the position of the cutoff line.

However, the actual results obtained from this system have been disappointing. During fiscal year 1974, there was an increase in the availability of funds in the state. Instead of shifting the cutoff line downward to include more marginal decision packages, Governor Carter requested new decision packages from some of his departments to help him allocate additional funds.

In fiscal year 1975 there was a reduction in the availability of funds originally projected for that year. Again, the decision-package ranking proved ineffective. Instead of raising the cutoff line to eliminate the lower priority decision packages, almost all departments had to resubmit a new decision-package ranking based on the lower level of funding. One departmental budget analyst summed up the problem by stating: "The priority ranking of our decision packages when we expect 140 percent funding simply is not the same as when we expect 115 percent funding."

Practicality of Preparing Decision Packages and Notification of Changes in Decision-Package Rankings

As used in this study, the term "decision package" is restricted to its application in a zero-base budgeting system. The Zero-Base Budgeting Manual of the state of Georgia defines a decision package as "an identification of a discrete function or operation in a definitive manner for management evaluation and comparison to other functions, including consequences of not performing that function, alternative courses of action, and cost and benefits."[14]

Decision packages differ from programs because of the time frames involved. A program includes the projected financial data applicable throughout the program's life; the financial data included in a decision package refer only to the fiscal year under consideration.

Decision packages are used in zero-base budgeting systems in both industry and government, although the format of the packages

TABLE 10.4

The Effects of Zero-Base Budgeting on the Reallocation of the State's Financial Resources as Perceived by Budget Analysts

	Departmental Budget Analysts		OPB Budget Analysts		Total	
	No.	Percent	No.	Percent	No.	Percent
Did the implementation of the zero–base budgeting system cause a shifting of financial resources among functions in your agency?						
Large shifting of financial resources.						
Some shifting of financial resources.	4	17.4	3	33.3	7	21.9
No apparent shifting of financial resources.	19	82.6	2	22.2	21	65.6
Uncertain.			4	44.5	4	12.5

Source: Compiled by the authors.

165

TABLE 10.5

Sample Decision Package, 1973 Fiscal Year Budget

Package Name	Agency	Activity	Organization	Rank
Air Quality Laboratory (1 of 3)	Health	Air Quality Control	Ambient Air	3

Statement of Purpose

Ambient air laboratory analysis must be conducted for identification and evaluation of pollutants by type and by volume. Sample analysis enables engineers to determine effect of control and permits use of an emergency warning system.

Description of Actions (Operations)

Use a central lab to conduct all sample testing and analysis: 1 Chemist II, 1 Chemist I, 2 Technicians, and 1 Steno I. This staff could analyze and report on a maximum of 37,300 samples. At 37,300 samples per year, we would only sample the 5 major urban areas of the state (70 percent of the population). These 5 people are required as a minimum to conduct comprehensive sample analysis of even a few samples on a continuous basis.

Achievement from Actions

Ambient air laboratory analysis yields valuable information for management and field engineers to enable them to evaluate effects of the Air Quality Program, identify new or existing pollutants by type and volume, and maintain an emergency warning system.

Consequences of Not Approving Package

Field engineers would be forced to rely on their portable testing equipment which does not provide the desired quantitative data (the portable equipment only identifies pollutants by major type, does not measure particle size, and does not provide quantitative chemical analyses to determine the specific chemical compounds in the pollutant), and greatly reduces the effectiveness of the emergency warning system which requires detailed quantitative chemical analyses.

166

Quantitative Package Measures	Fiscal Year 1971	Fiscal Year 1972	Fiscal Year 1973	Resources Required (dollars in thousands)	Fiscal Year 1971	Fiscal Year 1972	Fiscal Year 1973	Percent Fiscal Year 73/72
Samples analyzed & reported	38,000	55,000	37,300	Operational	160	224	140	63%
Cost per sample	$4.21	$4.07	$3.75	Grants				
Samples per man hour	3.8	3.9	3.7	Capital Outlay				
				Lease Rentals				
				Total	160	224	140	63%
				People (Positions)	5	7	5	71%

Manager _____ Prepared By _____ Date _____

Alternatives (Different Levels of Effort) and Cost

Air Quality Laboratory (2 of 3): $61K*—Analyze 27,700 additional samples (totaling 55,000 samples, which is the current level), thereby determining air quality for 5 additional problem urban areas and 8 other counties chosen on the basis of worst pollution (covering 80 percent of the population).

Air Quality Laboratory (3 of 3): $45K—Analyze 20,000 additional samples (totaling 75,000 samples), thereby determining air quality for 90 percent of the population, and leaving only rural areas with little or no pollution problems unsampled.

Alternatives (Different Ways of Performing the Same Function, Activity, or Operation)

Contract sample analysis work to Georgia Tech—Cost $6 per sample for a total cost of $224K for analyzing 37,300 samples. Emergency warning system would not be as effective due to their time requirement on reporting analysis work done by graduate students.

(continued)

Table 10.5, continued

Package Name	Agency	Activity	Organization	Rank
Air Quality Laboratory (1 of 3)	Health	Air Quality Control	Ambient Air	3

Conduct sample analysis work entirely in regional locations—cost a total of $506K the first year and $385K in subsequent years. Specialized equipment must be purchased in the first year for several locations if central lab is discontinued. Subsequent years would also require lab staffing at several locations at minimum levels which would not fully utilize people.

Conduct sample analysis work in central lab for special pollutants only, and set up regional labs to reduce sample mailing costs—cost a total of $305K for analyzing 37,300 samples. Excessive cost would persist due to minimum lab staffing at several locations in addition to the special central lab.

Source of Funds (dollars in thousands)	Fiscal Year 1971	Fiscal Year 1972	Fiscal Year 1973	Fiscal Year 1974	Fiscal Year 1975	Fiscal Year 1976	Fiscal Year 1977	Fiscal Year 1978
				Projection of Funds Committed by This Package	Funds			
					State			
					Total			
Operational: Other	Federal			Reasons:				
	State							
Grants:	Federal							
	State							
Capital and	Federal							
Lease:	State							

*$61K = $61,000.
Source: Compiled by the authors.

168

differs slightly between the two types of organizations. Table 10.5 is a sample of a decision package for use in the 1973 Fiscal Year Budget.

The preparation of decision packages is essential to the zero-base system. Each department or agency identifies various decision packages and the benefits expected, gives the costs of resources required, and lists the consequences of not funding the package (among other data). The packages then are ranked in order of decreasing benefit to the department or agency.

Responses of budget analysts regarding the practicality of preparing decision packages are given in Table 10.6. A total of 62.5 percent of all respondents and 74 percent of departmental budget analysts believed that it was not practical to prepare a decision package representing a minimum level of effort.

As for notification of changes in the rankings of decision packages at the executive level, 74 percent (see Table 10.6) said they were notified always or most of the time. It would seem desirable that notification always be given when changes in the rankings are made.

Future Use of Zero-Base Budgeting System

Table 10.7 presents a summary of the responses of budget analysts regarding the advisability of continuing the zero-base budgeting system in the state.

Of the respondents, 84 percent recommended the continued use of zero-base budgeting in some form. This is somewhat surprising because most of the preliminary interviews with budget analysts seemed to reveal a great deal of dissatisfaction with the new budgeting system. This dissatisfaction also was reflected, to a lesser degree, by the responses to various questions in the questionnaire.

While expressing dissatisfaction with many parts of the zero-base budgeting system, most analysts concede that there has been a basic improvement in the budgeting process as a result of implementing the new budgeting system. Also, the opinion was expressed that it was better to continue the present system rather than have to learn a new system or relearn the incremental budgeting system.

CONCLUSIONS

Three primary advantages appear to be associated with the employment of the zero-base budgeting system in the state of Georgia.

The first advantage concerns the establishment of a financial planning phase prior to the preparation of the fiscal year budget. Before

TABLE 10.6

Perceptions of Budget Analysts Regarding the Preparation and Notification of Changes in Ranking of Decision Packages

	Departmental Budget Analysts		OPB Budget Analysts		Total	
	No.	Percent	No.	Percent	No.	Percent
Presently you are required to prepare decision packages representing different levels of effort for each function. Do you feel it is practical to prepare a decision package representing a minimum level of effort?						
Yes.	6	26.1	5	55.6	11	34.3
No.	17	73.9	3	33.3	20	62.5
No opinion.			1	11.1	1	3.1
After your agency has submitted its decision-package rankings for executive review, are you notified of any changes in these rankings and the reasons for the change?						
Always.	8	34.8	2	25.0	10	32.3
Most of the time.	9	39.1	4	50.0	13	41.9
Seldom.	2	8.7	2	25.0	4	12.9
Never.	4	17.4			4	12.9

Source: Compiled by the authors.

TABLE 10.7

Opinions of Departmental Budget Analysts Regarding the Future Use of Zero-Base Budgeting

This study is very interested in your opinion of the zero-base budgeting system. Which of the following alternatives do you feel is in the best interest of the state of Georgia?

	Departmental Budget Analysts		OPB Budget Analysts		Total	
	No.	Percent	No.	Percent	No.	Percent
Continue the zero-base budgeting system substantially as it operates today.	5	21.7	5	55.6	10	31.3
Continue the zero-base budgeting system with some major modifications.	10	43.5	2	22.2	12	37.5
Continue the zero-base budgeting system except that it not be employed every year.	3	13.1	2	22.2	5	15.6
Discontinue the zero-base budgeting system.	5	21.7			5	15.6

Source: Compiled by the authors.

the implementation of zero-base budgeting, the planning phase was conducted concurrently with the budgeting phase. As a result, there were no budgetary guidelines available during the budget preparation. After the implementation of zero-base budgeting it became apparent that some budgetary guidelines were necessary to properly allocate the state's limited financial resources in such a way as to best satisfy the goals and objectives of the state.

The second advantage concerns an improvement in the quality of management information resulting from the employment of the zero-base budgeting system. The use of this new budgeting system has enabled the governor, department heads, departmental budget analysts, and budget analysts in the Office of Planning and Budget to have a much greater insight into the functions of state government.

The third advantage of employing the zero-base budgeting system has been an increase in the involvement of personnel at the activity level in the state's budgeting process. Before zero-base budgeting, most of the input into the budgeting process came from the departmental budget analysts. After the new budgeting system was implemented, activity managers were required to prepare and rank decision packages, thus providing input into the budgeting process.

The major disadvantage associated with the employment of the zero-base budgeting system in the state appears to be the increased time and effort required for budget preparation. This is a very serious problem, and it has contributed to some of the dissatisfaction with the new system, particularly among personnel at the department and activity level. This dissatisfaction, in turn, has had a detrimental effect on the effectiveness of the zero-base budgeting system. Quite possibly the amount of time and effort required will decrease significantly as all persons become more familiar with the new system.

The study indicates that there have been two other significant shortcomings associated with the employment of zero-base budgeting in the state of Georgia. These are: (1) the contention that the new budgeting system to date has not significantly affected the efficient allocation of the state's financial resources and (2) the seeming ineffectiveness of the decision-package ranking in meeting changes in the level of funding. However, the previous system also included these same shortcomings. Possibly, as those involved gain more experience in preparing and ranking decision packages, these shortcomings will be eliminated. On balance, the implementation of zero-base budgeting appears to have served the best interests of the state of Georgia.

NOTES

1. Peter A. Phyrr, "Zero-Base Budgeting," Harvard Business Review (November-December 1970): 111-21.

2. Jimmy Carter, State of the State Address, January 11, 1972, unpublished speech presented to the Joint Session of the General Assembly of Georgia, Atlanta, Georgia.

3. Ibid.

4. Jimmy Carter, Budget Address to the Joint Session of the General Assembly of Georgia, unpublished speech presented to the Joint Session of the General Assembly of Georgia, Atlanta, Georgia, January 13, 1972.

5. Ibid.

6. S. Kenneth Howard, "Changing Concepts of State Budgeting," Approaches to the State Central Budget Process (Lexington, Kentucky: National Association of State Budget Officers, 1970), p. 5.

7. Charles E. Lindblom, "Decision-Making in Taxation and Expenditure," Public Finances: Needs, Sources, and Utilization (Princeton, New Jersey: Princeton University Press, 1961), pp. 297-98.

8. Peter Phyrr, "Zero-Base Budgeting," unpublished speech delivered to the international conference of the Planning Executives Institute, New York Hilton Hotel, May 15, 1972.

9. U. S. Congress, Senate Committee on Government Operations, Subcommittee on National Policy Machinery, Hearings Organizing for National Security: The Budget and the Policy Process, 87th Congress, 1st Session, 1961, p. 1107.

10. Governor Jimmy Carter, interview held in the Governor's Office, State Capitol Building, Atlanta, Georgia, January 7, 1974.

11. Ibid.

12. Ibid.

13. Ibid.

14. Zero-Base Budgeting Manual—Fiscal Year 1973 Budget Development, State of Georgia (March 15, 1971), p. 2.

ABOUT THE EDITORS

JOHN A. WORTHLEY is associate professor of public administration at Long Island University, and a consultant to state, local, and federal agencies. A specialist in budgeting and information systems, he has been a Visiting Professor at SUNY Albany and Russell Sage College, and frequent lecturer at other universities , and was a financial adviser and faculty member at Briarcliff College. Worthley is the author of two books, and numerous articles in journals such as Public Administration Review, The Bureaucrat, and Western Political Quarterly, and is a member of the editorial board of the International Review of Public Administration. He currently is a widely used consultant to governments and private agencies involved with zero-base budgeting.

WILLIAM G. LUDWIN teaches public finance, budgeting, and economics at Indiana University-Purdue University at Fort Wayne. He holds a doctorate in public administration from SUNY Albany and has management experience in both the private and public sectors. He served on the staff of the Seventh Coast Guard District and held two management positions with the New York Telephone Company. He has published several articles on financial management and is a budgeting consultant to state and local governments.